JUNIOR'S HANDBOOK OF ESSAYS, LETTERS, PARAGRAPHS AND PRECIS WRITING

JUNIOR'S HANDBOOK OF ESSAYS, LETTERS, PARAGRAPHS AND PRECIS WRITING

A.K. CHATURVEDI

GOODWILL PUBLISHING HOUSE®
B-3 RATTAN JYOTI, 18 RAJENDRA PLACE
NEW DELHI - 110008 (INDIA)

Published by
GOODWILL PUBLISHING HOUSE®
B-3 Rattan Jyoti, 18 Rajendra Place
New Delhi-110008 (INDIA)
Tel. : 25750801, 25820556
Fax : 91-11-25764396
E-mail : goodwillpub@vsnl.net
website : www.goodwillpublishinghouse.com

Printed at : Kumar Offset Printers, Delhi-110092

AUTHOR'S NOTE

This book of English Composition in 'Different forms' has been prepared for the benefit of students of the Junior, Higher Secondary and Intermediate classes. It is very important that students of these classes must learn to write correct language in a correct form. Children, boys and girls, learn to speak English but when it comes to writing down, they fumble and falter. Spoken English can be learnt through constant contact with teachers, class-mates, even parents sometimes, who converse in English — that is particularly so in big and metropolitan cities — but not so in smaller towns, where the general atmosphere is not that English oriented. But even such boys and girls who seem to be talking fluently in English, when it comes to writing they find themselves in difficulty. Grammar and the grammatical rules; the correct use of words and phrases, is something that can come only through written practice. For this purpose it is necessary for them to have before them some models; it is necessary that they are made to know some rules, how to write what and how to write what to whom. Even writing down Essays on topics of common knowledge and interest is also found not that easy. How to rightly convert a Direct narration into an Indirect narration; how to think out points on a subject and compile them in the form of an Essay; how and what to write if putting in an application to the Principal for leave; how to place an order for books to a bookseller or a publisher and even how and what to write to one's friend inviting him to join you in a picnic. How to condense your thoughts in the minimum number of words — that also is a difficult exercise and students need to learn how to do so through Precis-writing exercises.

In this way, writing an Essay; expanding an idea; shortening ideas in the minimum number of words; drafting an application or an order for obtaining something — all these are the exercises in English Composition which have been tried to be covered in this small volume titled as 'Junior's Handbook of Essays, Letters, Paragraph and Precis Writing'. There are models of all forms given in this book and students down from class IV up to class XIII can find this book equally helpful for all standards in writing correctly, comfortably and cogently.

A.K. CHATURVEDI

CONTENTS

ESSAY WRITING

1. A POLICEMAN

The very name of a policeman evokes some sort of a fear. When a child goes on crying or does not go to sleep the mother would say "'don't cry' or 'Go to sleep soon' otherwise I would call the police'. The child can stop crying or would close his or her eyes as if going to sleep. This is how the very mention of a policeman can create a sense of fear even among children. If a policeman just comes and knocks at somebody's doors with his baton, those inside the house, if have got a peep from the window of the man in uniform, would shudder in their nerves as if it is a knock of some danger. To the village-folk a policeman just moving in the lanes of the village would be enough to create a flutter. Why only in the villages, a white-leveried traffic constable on the road crossing is such a symbol of authority. None dare ignore his signals, and if one ever does so even unintentionally or unconsciously, a raised finger of his has to make you stop by the side of the road till he comes to you. How much do the driver of the car, how very highly placed he be, would urge upon the man in uniform how he had inadvertently missed his signal and would be careful in future. An apology from the driver of the car can let him be off or else one may even have to dole out a good enough amount to let him go. You have to get lighter with your purse — really the most unfortunate aspect of our social order. Law should not be purchasable — this is what the young citizens of the country must learn, though it be learnt the hard way even at the risk of suffering some odds.

So a policeman is one who has been put in a uniform to enforce law and punish the wrong doer. If we all do the right actions, behave with others with calm and courtesy, we would hardly ever need the police-action. But that is what does not happen.

Everyday just as we open the first page of the newspaper, we get to find news of this crime and that crime; this dacoity or that kidnapping; this bag-snatching or that chain-snatching — gangs of autothieves operating or gangs of highwaymen looting the passenger buses. Even the so-called high ups of the society are found involved in shooting sprees or in murders and kidnappings for money or ransom or revenge.

In such a society where men are not law-abiding but rather are law-breakers, there needs to be some agency to catch the wrong doers and bring them to book. This is what the policeman does and this is why he has to be there. The wronged must have someone to go to with his complaint or with his tale of woe. He or she goes to the police station to lodge his or her complaint. One does go there in the hope that one would be heard, one's complaint recorded, investigated into and the wrong doer would be punished. This does not always happen, that is so unfortunate with our society.

But as long as the citizens keep on suffering crimes, policemen would be needed and it would indeed be a great day for our society if the policeman fulfils his obligations rightly and does his duty faithfully.

When that would happen a policeman would be treated as a friend and not one to be feared from. The presence of a policeman should create a sense of confidence and security.

POINTS TO REMEMBER

- The very name of a policeman creates a sense of fear.
- A policemen is meant to enforce law.
- If citizens behave calmly and courteously with one another, no policemen would be needed.
- Daily crimos are reported and the policeman becomes important.
- Policemen must do their duty faithfully. Then they would become public-friendly.

❑ ❑ ❑

2. THE POSTMAN

The Postman is the carrier of good and bad news. Letters sent by friends, relatives, wives to their husbands, parents to their children in far off towns are brought and delivered at our doors by the postman. Invitations for marriages, greetings on birthdays or anniversaries are sent by post and it is the post man who brings them to you. He also, sometimes, brings the bad news — the serious illness of a near and dear one, even the news of death.

A soldier posted on the heights of the Himalayas, on the snowy borders of our country has no other way to keep contact with his people in the far off towns or villages except through letters sent or received and the postman is the medium to bring these letters. How eagerly are these letters awaited on both ends.

Letters have not only the communicative value but they have a sentimental value too. This value cannot be replaced by any other means of communication. A hand written letter is a treasure for all times and a sweet remembrance of the writer who has long been dead and gone. Just open up the cupboard and draw out the packet of old letters, if they have been preserved and a rush of memories floats along before the mind's eye. Who did bring them? — the postman of course.

These days the importance of handwritten letters is getting reduced and so is the importance of the postman. The new means of communication —the E-mails; the faxes; the internet chatting — all these are replacing the handwritten letters. People take the excuse of being too busy — 'machines' have taken over the 'man' in human relationship. A minutes 'Hello' 'Hello' on the telephone fulfils all the obligations of inter-communication. Who would now undertake any research on the letters written by Jawaharlal Nehru to his daughter Indira Gandhi? Who would get the pleasure of probing into the sentiments of Keats — the great English poet — contained in his letters to his beloved and friends or Lord Chesterton sending his advices to his son. Those were handwritten letters having a historical, sentimental and personal value. And all these letters must have been delivered by the postman.

A village postman is still very important in our country. He does not only carry letters but he even pens down the replies of the illiterate parents or a comely unlettered lass to her husband. The postman has to inscribe in words the message of blessings or love. He plays a great role — without him, the surging feelings of the heart would have remained uncommunicated.

Lesser in demand, though, but the role of the postman has ever been and shall ever remain a real role in communicating the heart to the heart; the mind to the mind. Business would come to a stand still if documents and commitments are not sent and received. Who else to carry the written and signed word — of course and indeed the Postman.

POINTS TO REMEMBER

- The Postman has ever been the carrier of the good and the bad news.
- It is the postman who is the only means of communication between the soldier on the country's snowy borders and his parents or his wife in the far off town or village.
- Handwritten letters have not only a communicative value but a sentimental, even a historical value and these have been delivered only through the medium of the postman.
- Importance of handwritten letters and consequently of the postman has been reduced — there have developed other mechanical means of communications.
- A village postman is still very important as he carries letters as also pens down replies from illiterate parents or wives.
- The postman shall remain important as he carries and delivers business documents and deeds from one end to another. Without him all business would come to a standstill.

3. OUR PETS — DOGS AND CATS

Keeping pets is also a pleasant hobby. A dog has ever been a favourite pet with people. There is a quite a reason for this choice. A dog is a very faithful and loving a pet as well as a great watchful creature. People keep a dog as a pet for reasons — a liking for them as also a constant watchman by night and day. There are sign boards at the gate of persons keeping dogs as pets 'Beware of dogs' which means that the dogs kept as pets would not allow any unknown person to enter the premises of the house. This is a great advantage and a great protection. There are different species of dogs, some are just lovely, furry, fluffy beings who sit crouched cosily in the lap — harmless ones — harmless even to an outsider. There are the other ones who are the bigger ones in size and ferocious indeed. They can tear an intruder apart, would bark aloud to awaken the whole house. They may be ferocious to an outsider or an intruder but to their master and to the family they are docile and cool — abiding by their every command or direction. The master and the dog are the inseparable when the master is back home after his day's work. It must jump up to reach the master, feel a contentment only after being given a loving pat, not without it. Faithful they are to that extent that stories go about some of them who gave up food and drink and gave up their lives after their master was no more.

Dogs have a great instinct of learning. Though animals, they exhibit a great sense of intelligence. They can be trained even by the crime-investigating agencies and have successfully worked out to catch the criminal.

Loving, faithful, ferocious and intelligent with an instinct to learn — that is all about dogs as pets.

Cats are kept as pets too. But as contrasted with dogs cats are less faithful, less loving more self-loving. They cannot be any risk to an intruder and can be lured away.

There have been no cases of cats sacrificing themselves for their master. But they are lovely creatures who would cosily comfort themselves in the bed of their masters and love to be in the lap. People keep cats as pets just for their looks — their fluffy purring behaviour. They are loved for their looks — that is what cats are.

Keeping pets is both a pleasure and a task. Once one gets lured to keep pets, one cannot give up one's liking for them, so much so that pets -- dogs and cats — once kept, they become a part of the family, a part of life and one cannot give them up. It is a love that lasts.

POINTS TO REMEMBER

- Pets — keeping is a pleasant hobby.
- Dogs are kept as pets both for liking as well as for protection.
- Dogs are very faithful pets — ferocious for intruders but most caring and loving for the family.
- Dogs have the instinct to learn, if trained.
- Cats do not have those loving and faithful qualities. They care for themselves.
- Keeping pets is a pleasure as well as a task — a hobby which once developed cannot easily be given up.

4. MAN IS THE BEST OF GOD'S CREATION

Shakespeare makes the hero Hamlet of his play 'Hamlet' say, 'what piece of work is a man'. What has been said by Hamlet is really a great truth. Man is the best of God's creation. He is the best being among the living creatures. Man is the only one among God's creations who is a 'thinking' being. So far as his physical behaviour is concerned, man is just like an animal; eating, drinking, sleeping. But man also has reason — he has the thinking capacity — he can reason out things, he can argue, he can hold his views and convince others of his views or get convinced from the views of others. Man has been able to develop and create so many new things and keeps on inventing, creating and discovering newer and newer things. This only the man can do. If this has not been so man would have remained a savage as he was in primitive days.

Man above can feel — animals also feel but their feeling is instinctive not as a result of any thought.

Man is also a social being. From the Stone age, he came up to the Iron age and from the iron age he grew into a move civilised being. He began to live together with his fellows — villages came into existence, then towns, then big cities, then metropolitan towns. Man created machines and factories grew, markets came into existence. Man began to travel — cars, buses, trucks, trains, aeroplanes were invented and it is man alone who can thus travel from one place to another. Means of transport developed to such an extent that man could travel even upto the moon and set his foot on that planet. Unthinkable and unimaginable feats have been performed by man and it is only because man is able to think and plan and turn his plans into reality.

Man can now fly in the air like birds, travel over the seas and oceans, go deep down into the depths of the ocean or earth and explore the unexplored. Now he can communicate with his friends and his family thousands of miles away on telephone, E-mail, fax and do the chatting on the internet. He has written down his thoughts in the form of books and thus the human thought has been and can be preserved for times immemorial.

Even in the field of warfare the nuclear bombs, the unmanned missiles can strike targets thousands of miles away.

In the field of physical well being, man has invented medicines for most of the diseases, he has even successfully designed and made artificial lungs and hopes to develop artificial heart.

How very wonderful are man's achievements but it would be the best if all these achievements are used in human welfare and social well-being and not for any destructive means. That would really make man 'the wonderful being of God's creation'.

POINTS TO REMEMBER

- Man is the best creation among God's creatures.
- Man is a 'thinking' being which no other creature is.
- He has thought and planned and has created, invented and discovered newer and newer things.
- Man is the only creature who has a feeling and that has made him into a social being.
- Even the unimaginable things have been created by man. He can fly in the air, go over the seas and oceans and has even been able to reach the moon.
- In the field of warfare very deadly weapons have been invented. Factories and mills have been built.
- But man would really be the best of the creations if everything that he creates is for the welfare of the fellow-beings.

5. FRIENDS AND FRIENDSHIP

Man has slowly and gradually grown into a social being. This is what has been the result of man becoming a civilised being. Man has feelings and these feelings bring him closer to one another — they need companionship and communion. Talking and laughing are qualities which only man possesses. But for these actions man needs some company to talk to, laugh with. Men of the same taste, of the same temper began coming closer and this resulted in the concept of friends and friendship. 'Birds of the same feather flock together' — this is how the saying goes and this is the basis and the background of friends and friendship. Those who are of similar tastes come closer and become companions.

Friendship is a nice thing in social life. But it would be nicer of this continues throughout life. That is what, sometimes, does not happen. It is not always necessary that when a group, on whatever basis it gets formed, shall continue to remain adjusted and adjoined. Men are generally selfish and self-centred. And as soon as the self-interest of one comes in conflict with the other, even long-standing friendships break away and groups disintegrate.

Therefore friendship is a difficult venture and can only remain in tact when friends are prepared to sacrifice their self-interest for the sake of others; when they are prepared to serve others even risking one's own safety and interest. This needs a strong will power and a sense of sacrifice which is a very rare quality among people.

A friend in need is a friend indeed — this is how the saying about friendship goes. Real friendship is tested only during the period of distress and crisis. When we are faced with difficulty and are at the edge of disaster then is the true test of a real friend. If one comes to render help in this hour even at his personal risk then would it be that one would be the real friend. Otherwise, what is generally seen that so long as one is in a state of prosperity and pelf there would be many who would gather around the enjoy but the moment distress falls, slowly and gradually most of them walk away. Such are known as 'fair-weather' friends.

Therefore, great care has to be taken in choosing friends. Even a fake test can put a friend on trial — that is what may be done.

It is not always necessary that friendship may grow only among people of equal status. Lord Krishna, the King of Dwarka could have a close friend in a poor pauper — Sudama. That is a great example of real friendship.

Real friendship is that which is sustained and continued in all times and in all circumstances. This is what is found difficult but is the most desired.

POINTS TO REMEMBER

- With the growth of civilisation man has become a social being. He needs company and companionship.
- People of the same taste and temper generally come together and form a group of friends.
- Friendship is a difficult venture. Self-interest coming in conflict breaks friendships.

- Friendship can continue only when friends are prepared to sacrifice their self-interest for the sake of the other.
- 'A friend in need is the friend indeed'. An hour of need is the testing time of friendship.
- It is not always necessary that men should have equal social status to become good friends. Lord Krishna and Sudama are the great example.

❑ ❑ ❑

6. DISCIPLINE

Whether it is the society or the home or the school, discipline is the watchword every where. Men who live in the society need to follow some rules and regulations which help in running life smoothly — this is what is called discipline. For the running of any organisation or institution it is necessary to frame some rules and the primary and essential need to run it well is to follow those rules. Those who are members of such an organisation or institution also feel a sense of pride that they belong to a disciplined body.

The army, or the police have to be the most disciplined force. When on January 26 at the Republic Day parade in our country how elegant it looks when the army contingent or the police force marches with symmetrical steps. It is only the training in discipline that makes them to move in this manner. For the men of the armed forces the watchword is 'It's not to question why it's but to do or die'. This is the sense of discipline with which our country's borders and our nations honour are being protected by our army.

On the play field all the players have to follow the rules of the game and they cannot question the authority of the umpire and have to quietly submit to his decision. In the classroom the teacher's orders have to be obeyed only then can the teaching be conducted properly. You cannot indulge in mutual jokes or make noise while the teacher is teaching. Total attention to what the teacher is teaching calls for discipline. The teacher has also to maintain a certain decorum while teaching. He cannot tell stories instead of teaching the lesson.

But to follow discipline one has to limit and curtail his own liberty. You have the liberty to dress in whatever manner you please but if there is a particular dress prescribed by the school authorities, you have to put on that dress during school hours.

While moving on the road the rule of the road is that you move on your left. If this rule is not followed, there would be all confusion and accidents.

In life also there has to be some discipline. Break the rules of nature in food and drink — the result would be ill-health. The family functions on discipline. The child must listen to what the mother and the father say. The brother must have the regard for the brother and the sister. Mutual respect and regard is the discipline of a home.

Therefore, whether it is the social life, whether it is a club or a school or a home — rules have to be followed — and that is discipline. without that there would be all chaos and confusion.

POINTS TO REMEMBER

- Discipline is the watch word everywhere — whether society, school, an organisation or home.

- Army and the police force are based on discipline. Orders must be obeyed.
- So it is in the school; in the classroom — full attention to the teacher.
- To follow discipline, one's personal liberty has to be curtailed — whether it is moving on the road or living in a family.
- Even in general life the rules of nature if broken would mean ill-health.
- Discipline is the key word for a smooth system of life.

7. COURTESIES COST NOTHING BUT PAYS A LOT

'Little drops of water make the mighty ocean'.

A drop of water in itself might appear to be meaningless but gathered together one by one — and the mighty ocean is formed. What is an ocean but a collection of drops. So are the clouds, but they cover the entire sky on a rainy day.

This is what is true of courtesies. 'Please let me go' — you say in a crowded place and there who form the crowd give you the passage and you in return say 'Thank you so much'. What did you lose or what did 'Please' and 'Thank you' cost you but you have won the goodwill. You help an old man cross a busy road and he blesses you with all his heart. You did not know him, he did not know you but the show of the little courtesy by you have got you a store of blessings and blessings from elders mean a lot.

You are moving in a crowded market place and tread upon somebody's foot. Immediately you say 'So Sorry, have hurt you?' The man's foot though might have been hurt but he would just pat you on the shoulder and say 'no, nothing, young man'. What did it cost you to say 'Sorry' but you won the goodwill of the other man.

So the smooth functioning of the social life goes on only on mutual courtesies.

We call ourselves highly civilised. But being civilised does not mean living in posh bungalows and driving costly cars and dancing at clubs and having dinners at hotels. Being civilised means how you behave with your fellow social beings. Everyday you read in the newspapers how a youngman of a so-called high family shot down a bar-maid for not serving him liquor past midnight, or a youngman kidnaps and murders another youngman out of malice. Such youngmen belonging to the so-called 'high families' are hardly civilised — they are boorish and brute. They do not have even the primary lessons in courtesy or correct conduct.

Live with love and conduct yourself with consideration for others — that makes life in the society worthy of living and you a worthy member of it.

A.G. Gardiner — an English essayist writes in one of his essays — "'Please' and 'Thank you' are like little drops of oil which help the machine of life run smooth". These little courtesies are like rain drops which make the face of nature shine up — the clouds do not ask anything in return for what they do.

POINTS TO REMEMBER

- Little courtesies are like little drops of water — to make the mighty ocean of social life.

- 'Please' and 'Thank you' are little phrases which receive immediate positive reaction.
- So is the word 'Sorry' for any harm done to anybody unintentionally.
- Being civilised means being courteous. Big bungalows and big cars do not define being civilised.
- Mutual love, sympathy and respect make the society a worthy place to live and make a man a worthy citizen.

❐ ❐ ❐

8. ARE WE HAPPIER THAN OUR FOREFATHERS ?

To deal with this subject one must first understand what 'happiness' means.

We have not to misunderstand 'pleasure' with 'happiness'. A lavish life style, a rich home a big bungalow and a luxurious car — these are today treated as the means of 'happiness'. We are very 'happy' if we have all these. But it is such a mistaken belief. All these are 'pleasures' and 'comforts' of life. Physical comforts are the mirage which give a false sense of 'happiness'. Man has three parts of his being — the physical, the mental and the spiritual. Physical comforts are the lowest in the ladder. Healthy thoughts, right behaviour give one the mental well-being. Serving others, being good to people, gives one an miner solace and satisfaction — that is a spiritual well being.

So here lies the difference between 'pleasure' and 'happiness'. To have a lot of eat and drink is all enjoying the pleasures of life.

A hermit living in a hut may have so much of self-satisfaction. He serves people who go to him with words of high thoughts and advice on worthy living. He is a man in rags, eats whatever he gets as charity, still he is 'happy'. He does not have the 'pleasures' of life but he has the 'happiness' of his mind and soul.

We today have everything at our command, Science is at our beck and call. We have all the comforts of life which our ancestors never could even dream of. Means of transport, means of communication, means of entertainment — Cinema, T.V. with so many channels — phones, E-mails, Fax, Internet — what not. Still if you ask even the richest of men if he is really 'happy', he may just shake his head to show 'no, not that'. There are worries, there are anxieties, there is no sense of satisfaction or contentment.

Men of the past had little but they lived all in a joint family serving each other, one another in their needs — sharing whatever they could produce or earn. They lived a life of frugality but contentment. They worked hard and could have a sound sleep at night. The home housed cousins, brothers, uncles, aunts all under one roof. Now there are two room cubicles in large busy towns — no space even for parents to come and stay. There had been an affectionate bond binding all in the past; there is a distance now even among the brothers. 'What is this life so full of care' — is what can be said of today's living.

Happiness comes from within. It is a sense if contentment which comes from the core of the heart. There is a couplet in Hindi which when translated says —

'All the wealth — cows, elephant, horses — and all the jewels — their treasure.

Nothing equals contentment — everything turns meaningless in measure.'

It is this contentment which is the basis of 'Happiness' and it is this that lacks in today's life while that was there is the past.

That tilts the balance of 'Happiness' in favour of our anscestors.

POINTS TO REMEMBER

- It is necessary first to understand what is 'Happiness'.
- Let us not mistake 'Pleasures' with 'Happiness'.
- Physical comforts do not and cannot give 'Happiness'.
- 'Happiness' is a state of mind which comes from contentment.
- Men of the past lived together, lived for one another, worked hard and slept soundly. They were contented with their lot.
- Even the richest man of today is not contented.
- Wealth and riches cannot bring 'Happiness' — mind and soul are its seat .
- Our ancestors enjoyed that 'Happiness' which we today fail to find.

❑ ❑ ❑

9. PARENTS AS FRIENDS

In the matter of the overall growth of a child the parental care has a very important part to play. Lack of this care results in children falling a prey to all the social ills that the modern society is wrought with. Neglected at home the growing mind of the child seeks company and companionship. Watching shows on the T.V. which these days, mainly expose crime, and sex, the little child begins to think that this is the way of normal life. All this leaves a very unhealthy effect on the child's mind.

Where mothers remain busy in kitty parties and fathers busy with the offices or their business, what are children to do ? After spending five to six hours at school, while at home they crave for company. Books cannot engage them for all times. As they step out of the house, there are gangsters and drug-traffickers ready and waiting to catch them as their parents have big money and the children have big pocket money available to them. Servants and 'ayahs' are as bad a company for these young rich.

The newspaper reports that a young boy, still in his teens, son of a man in position, goes to his friend in the afternoon, and asks him to come along with him. The friend just says, 'I'm not feeling well, I would not come' — and in utter disgust this young caller fires a bullet from a pistol which he carries — the bullet fortunately strikes the wall. What does this show? What mental frustration and disgust does this exhibit? This perverted mindset of the young is only because he suffers a neglect at home.

What is needed and is most necessary is that parents should be friends to their children. Even while at work they should keep contacting their children at home on phone, knowing from them what they did at school, how went their day, what is there in the fridge that they should eat; what they were to get from the father or the mother in the evening when they come back home. Such intimate and concerning enquiries even on a phone makes the child feel so good. He thinks that there are his parents caring for him and that is a great satisfaction to the child. He feels a sense of companionship and need not seek it elsewhere. When back at home in the evening, the father and the mother should spend most of their time with their children, play with them, cut jokes with them; tell stories to them and ask children to tell their stories about how they spend their day at school. Parents need not be overbearing and too sombre — they need to be close and friendly — children may find in them a true companion — a friend — a true confidant. This would provide to the child all the mental food for company which he or she craves for and makes him or her at peace within. Never would he be led to seek company elsewhere. This parental attention is a cure and a tonic to the growing mind in the otherwise, tense and tattered social life in today's world.

Let the parents awake to this consciousness and act accordingly. That would get rid them of so many problems with their children and relieve children also of unwanted influences.

POINTS TO REMEMBER

- Parental care has a long way to help in the mental growth of the child.
- Ever busy parents make children suffer from a sense of neglect.
- Such sense of neglect makes them seek company outside their homes and make them easy victims to undesirable social elements.
- Frustration and neglection at home give rise to a sense of frustration which may even lead to crime.
- Parents should act as friends to their children — be their companions while at home in the evenings and be their confidants in all matters.
- This relationship would save parents from so many children-related problems and save children from falling in bad company.

10. A GOOD CITIZEN

A citizen is not one who stays in a city. A citizen can even be one who stays in a village or in slums. One who is a member of the society — of whatever status, is a 'citizen'.

As a social being every citizen has his responsibilities towards the society. Every society wants its citizens to be good, and it is the goodness of the citizens which makes the society good.

History tells how during the reign of Chandra Gupta Maurya, people did not need to lock their doors. No thefts would be committed; no robberies ever did occur. May be that it was due to the stern administration and strict policing but it does reflect the nature of the society. All men were law-abiding and law fearing. There was peace and comfort.

Today in the same India, every morning the newspaper's front page news are there of dacoity, murder, kidnapping, and frauds. This picture of the society reflects the character of the citizens. To what low level have they fallen.

Just as to be healthy, every part of the body has to be healthy and in good condition. Similarly for the society to be good, every citizen has to be well-mannered, honest in his dealings, hard working in his pursuits.

What is meant by being a good citizen? The answer is not far to seek. A good citizen is one who is humble, polite to others, well-mannered, respectful to the feelings of others. 'Do not do unto others what you do not want to be done to you' — this is a mental dictate that governs a good citizen. What hurts you can hurt others too, therefore do not do anything to others which if done to you may hurt you. A society which works on these lines shall have citizens following this rule and that is good citizenship.

Everyone wants to have his personal freedom. But personal freedom does not give one the licence to do whatever one pleases. If you have the right to enjoy personal freedom others also have the right to enjoy the similar freedom. The freedom of one has to be accommodated with the freedom of others. Mutual adjustments alone can bring about peace in the society.

Therefore, a good citizen has always to take care of the interests of others. Neighbourly relations means caring for one another; helping others in the time of their need and be helped by others in your time of need.

It is such a society that everyone wants to live in. But to make the society so liveable every citizen must contribute his 'goodness'.

POINTS TO REMEMBER

- A citizen is not one who lives in the cities. Everyone living in the society is a 'citizen'.
- Every citizen has responsibilities towards the society.
- A good society would be that which has good citizens.
- A healthy body is that in which every part of the body is healthy.
- Who is a good citizen? One who cares for others, does not harm others; is humble and respects the sensibilities of others — such a one is a good citizen.

- Every one wants personal freedom but personal freedom cannot be unrestricted. Personal freedom of others must also be taken into consideration.
- Good of all — that sense and consideration is the basis of good citizenship.

❑ ❑ ❑

11. MY FAVOURITE TEACHER

Mr. Vaidya is my favourite teacher. Actually he is a favourite teacher not only mine but of a majority of students of the school. It is his kind, consideration and loving attitude towards his students which makes him such a favourite of all. He is so caring and so concerned about all and every body and about their problems.

"How are you? What is wrong with you? Why are you so upset, let me know?" These were the words which showed Mr. Vaidya's concern for me. I told him, "Sir, today is the last date for depositing my fees and form for my final examination. If I don't do it, my year would get wasted. I have not received the moneyorder sent a week back by my father — what am I to do" — and tears rolled down my cheeks. Mr. Vaidya patted me on my back, 'Oh, so that is the only thing — good boy, do not get that upset for such a small thing" and he opened up his purse and handed over the me required amount for the fees. It was such a relief to me and I just touched his feet expressing my heartfelt gratefulness. 'I will return the money as soon as I receive the moneyorder, Sir' — I said so and immediately Mr. Vaidya said "No, boy, don't worry, you've been such a good student. You must do well at the examination — your bright result would be the return of my money — work hard and top the list" — and Mr. Vaidya once again patted my back. How deeply touched did I feel.

It is not that Mr. Vaidya felt concerned about me. He has the concern for all his students. He takes personal interest in solving even the family problems of his students. The father of a student suffered an accident and had to be admitted to the hospital. Mr. Vaidya came to know of it and he was there at the hospital to visit the patient and make anxious enquiries about his health. One of his old students was the surgeon at the hospital. He particularly contacted him to ask him to look after the father of the boy with special care. Mr. Vaidya's old student, the surgeon had all the regard for his old teacher — his respected teacher.

If while waiting for the bus at the bus-stand, it began to drizzle, Mr. Vaidya would open up his umbrella and ask students standing there to come under it. How much concern he has for the welfare of his students — really a great man Mr. Vaidya is.

It was not only this human side of his that made Mr. Vaidya a favourite teacher. As a teacher of his subject, he was the best. He knew his subject so well and more than that the way he explained the difficult topics in such a lucid way, which made him such a respected teacher. He would never be late in coming to his class and would straightway begin with the lesson of the day — he may cut some pleasant jokes, sometimes — but would never indulge in telling unwanted stories. He never wasted any minute of his and students listened to him in rapt attention.

It was all that respect for him which made students so attentive and disciplined. He never had any problem with that.

Incidentally this was my last year at the school and Mr. Vaidya was also retiring the same year. At the close of the session after the final examinations were over, a grand farewell party was arranged by the students and teachers. The Principal, in his speech paid glowing tributes to Mr. Vaidya for the qualities of his head and heart. Students who came to speak — their voice choked with emotion; words failed them and at the close of the function there was such a rush of students coming up to touch Mr. Vaidya's feet to receive his blessings. Mr. Vaidya himself was full of emotion on this last day of his at the school which he had served with such a dedication and devotions.

That was Mr. Vaidya who else can be more favourite a teacher than he.

POINTS TO REMEMBER

- Mr. Vaidya is my favourite teacher — not only mine but of all the students.
- He has a genuine concern for his students and look after even their personal problems — paying the fees of students if that was needed or visiting an ailing father of a student in the hospital.
- As a teacher he knows his subject well and taught with great attention and clarity. No problem of discipline in his class.
- At the farewell party on his retirement the Principal praised the qualities of his head and heart and students rushed to touch his feet to receive his blessings.

12. AN IDEAL SCHOOL

An ideal school is that where the child is treated and cared for like a nascent plant. It is the plant which has to grow healthy. It should be properly manured and watered and also protected from sun and shade.

This is what an ideal school has to do with its little children. It is the child's physical as well as mental growth about which the school should remain concerned. Along with this, there should be all the attention paid to the moral development of the child. He should be given training in right conduct, right behaviour and noble thoughts. It is through lessons in the classroom as well as lessons in the campus that such a training can be given.

The ideal school should have proper arrangements in the classrooms — clean and well-arranged furniture and proper ventilation. For the nursery classes there should be charts and maps and pictorial presentation. A child learns more by seeing than by teaching. Musical rhymes in simple words give to the little child an instant appeal. They can hear and learn.

The campus of the school should also be clean and well-kept. Gardens and flowers and lawns present an agreeable atmosphere or if not all these at least a well cleaned area all around.

Then there should be arrangements for games and physical exercises for which special classes and periods be allotted.

The development of the body is as important as the development of the mind and an ideal school has to look after the part of child's physical development.

The classroom teaching should also be properly looked after and for this part an ideal school has to take great care in having teachers who are really devoted to their job — they need rather to be dedicated, and disciplined. They should know their job and should know what they have to teach and how to make the lesson enjoyable. A school which fails to have dedicated teachers, fails to come to the standard of an ideal school.

For this, it is necessary too that teachers be paid due regard. Their job is to build the society but for that it is equally necessary that they be paid well and be duly respected. With a sense of self-respect within them they can give their best. Along with this it has to be seen that a teacher who takes up his job indifferently has no right to be there is an ideal school.

The school should have a good library and students should be given a training in using the library to add to their general knowledge.

The library is the mental treasure of a school and students should draw out from it as much as they can.

Extra curricular activities are also an important and integral part of the school education. They give to students a nice exposure to develop their personality and provide them a forum to develop self-confidence. The main performers in these activities should be students — teachers should be only guiding them.

So many aspects, if properly looked after can made up an ideal school.

Last but not the least, children should be given due lessons in their moral and cultural background. They should be made to feel proud of their history and their culture — without this all education would be ill-bred and half-backed.

POINTS TO REMEMBER

- An ideal school takes every care of the growth of a child — physical, mental and moral.
- Training in right conduct and noble thoughts should be what an ideal school needs to give training in.
- An ideal school should have properly arranged classrooms and a clean campus — if possible with garden and flowers.
- Arrangement for games and physical exercises should be there.
- Teachers should be devoted and dedicated, should know their job and should be well-paid. Indifferent teachers should not be there.
- Good library and extra curricular activities are both an important item in an ideal school.
- Last but not the least, children should be given proper understanding of their culture and history — that an ideal school has to take care of.

❑ ❑ ❑

13. BOOKS — AS THE BEST COMPANION

One needs a companion to pass one's time; talk and play with the companion. But one cannot keep talking and playing all the time. And then all companions are not good company. There can be some who have bad habits and they would like others also to form the same habits. It is not, therefore, proper to have such companions and one should always avoid them.

The best, therefore is, to make books one's companions. As and when one has spare time, particularly during long holidays, one should take advantage of the companionship of books. They give one good lessons; they contain stories about great men how they became great. One knows about their lives and their lessons. Even small stories from 'Panchtantra' or the 'Aesop's Fables' or the story of the 'Ramayan' or the story of 'Mahabharat' or the pictorial stories of 'Amar Chitra Katha' can give one so much to know about the ancient scriptures and our great culture. Or even the stories written by other great writers or the life-histories of great men have so much to teach and one has so much to learn from them. Words of wisdom, noble thoughts, great deeds — this is what one gets from such books.

Instead of wasting time with friends, chatting on the films that might have been seen by them or watching the T.V. all the time would be a vain exercise. Newer and newer books with newer and newer ideas can be a great experience in learning the best about life.

Friends can even quarrel; they can even turn away and break the friendship but books can be a permanent companion. And then what is contained in a book always remains the same. Friend may change their mood but books shall always be the same. A good book shall always be good.

But one has to be careful in choosing books — what to read and what not to read. Books are also of different types — only the best have to be chosen. For choosing books worthy of companionship advice of teachers and elders be taken. They would always give the right advice and one must follow their advice in the matter.

The writers of good books give the best of their thoughts in the books written by them. To have such books as companions is to have the best thoughts as companions. Nothing can be worthier than that. It would be the best use of one's time.

POINTS TO REMEMBER

- One needs a companion to pass one's time.
- Companions and friends can even be such who have bad habits.
- Books with noble thoughts shall always be noble — they can be the best friends.
- Friends can even quarrel and turn away but a book always remains the same.
- It is necessary to choose good books as companions and in choosing them advice of teachers and elders be taken.
- Great writers give their best in their books and what else can be better than to be in the company of such great thoughts.

❑ ❑ ❑

14. POLLUTION

We find everyone everywhere talking about pollution — pollution of air, water, food and everything. When we try to study this problem of pollution we find that we ourselves are responsible for causing this pollution. People, in general, do not take care to keep their surroundings clear and this leads to general pollution. And this pollution causes ill-health and give rise to so many health problems.

Recently there has been a drive to convert the buses and the three-wheelers running in Delhi from diesel driven to CNG. Why was this large scale change found necessary? The reason was that with the rise in the population, the number of buses and three-wheelers also increased. The diesel-driven buses and three-wheelers emit smoke which goes into the atmosphere and the air. This smoke contains very unhealthy gases. People breathe this air. The result is that their lungs inhale these polluted gases within which causes so many lung diseases — even leading to bronchitis, asthma and tuberculosis. The rise in these diseases led the government to think and this led to this policy of converting these vehicles into CNG. Ever since this has been done the proportion of air pollution has largely decreased.

Then there is water pollution. The water we drink is lifted from the rivers, stored and then sent to us through pipe lines. What is happening to these rivers? Those rivers which used to be called our 'holy' rivers — Ganga and Yamuna — receive all the sewage from the city drains and so large a quantity of this sewage is that the river is not able to carry it away. The river water gets all polluted with all the filth that falls into it and it is this water that is pumped to the city's water-tanks. Even the underground water is becoming polluted as the filth and garbage over the earth seeps down when it rains and the underground water also gets polluted. All the lakes, ponds and even the wells of today contain polluted water. The large scale industries which are growing in large numbers to meet the demands of the growing population send out effluents which fall in the rivers, lakes and ponds and make their water unworthy of drinking.

People are cutting down trees. This is because, more population, more need of fuel and timber. Trees emit oxygen by day which purifies the atmosphere — loss of trees means loss of oxygen — the healthy gas.

Even too much use of fertilizers and pesticides in our farming process is also a cause of atmospheric pollution.

As we go around a town we find big heaps of garbage with all the rotting material. All this has been heaped by us — we are responsible for it. But this rotting sends up gases which mix in the air and pollute the atmosphere. We get rid of the garbage from our homes but make the whole neighbourhood polluted. The civic sense is lacking the civic authorities also are not able to make proper arrangement of garbage disposal.

Even the plastic bags, so much in use these days, are a cause of pollution as these are thrown away and do not get destroyed, but are recycled. The recycled plastic bags are very dangerous for health — any eatable kept in them turns unhealthy.

The growth of slums in big towns are a great source of pollution. People live in the most unhealthy surroundings, commit all sorts of nuisances and all this causes atmospheric pollution.

The problem of pollution is growing every day and is causing a risk to the population of the country.

What is necessary is that not only the administration but people in general must understand the gravity of this problem and each one should do his best to keep the atmosphere clean. Plant more trees; dispose off the garbage in the proper way. Keep the rivers clean, do not allow unhealthy ways of life to grow — it is each and every man's job to save the country from pollution.

POINTS TO REMEMBER

- Everything in our country is getting polluted — atmosphere, air, water, food.
- We ourselves are responsible for causing this pollution.
- The effort made in Delhi to convert buses and three-wheelers to CNG is a good beginning and has shown results.
- Water pollution is another major problem. Rivers are turning into sewages and water for drinking is becoming poisoned.
- Garbage heaps carried down under the earth by rain water is making even the underground water polluted.
- Cutting down of trees is cutting down oxygen — a purifier of atmosphere.
- The plastic bags thrown away after use never get destroyed and add to pollution.
- The growth of slums and unhealthy living conditions in them is a great cause of pollution.
- Each and everyone of us must tackle this problem, then alone it can be solved. The government alone cannot do it.

❑ ❑ ❑

15. SLUMS — WHY AND WHAT?

Slums around and within the big towns are a growing problem of our country. People migrating from the villages, attracted by the glamour of town life; come to the towns with no roof over their heads, no habitation to keep them in door. They take up odd jobs — rickshaw pulling, vegetable selling or any such job that comes their way and then where to stay, what to do? They gather together some pieces of wool or cardboards, encroach upon a piece of land found lying vacant, raise semblance of walls and cover them with pieces of cloth or anything that they find, sack or rags or plastic sheets and that becomes their home. Two, three or even four share that so-called habitation. This is how one after the other such shanties rise up, cluster together and form into a slum. Gradually with some money earned, they manage to instal a hand pump, or even take a water connection from the nearby pipe line, use the adjoining open fields as their toilets, cook their own meals after the days labour or before their day begins and thus goes on their life — this is how slums grow and this is why they come up. Once they come up, one after the other, here, there, everywhere, the political big-wings turn them into their vote-banks and then who can uproot them. They develop a political clout.

The story of slums goes on like this — they are here, there and all around in big cities and now have begun to develop within and around even smaller towns. They are a slur on our society — everyone knows it, even the highest in the authority know it and slowly and gradually efforts begin being made to regularise them, to legalise their unauthorised occupation.

Why should such slums come up? The reason is that population, particularly in the rural areas is fast increasing. The population there have no family-planning programme for their families. The agricultural land with a family remains the same while the mouths to be fed have grown. How to feed these additional mouths? This needs additional income. No industries or occupations are growing in the rural sector — the country's economic policy being lopsided, it is concentrating on large scale industrialisation. These need labour — the needy villager is quick to be a cheap labour and gets drawn to the town.

The townlife has its added attractions — more entertainment, more avenues of recreation — once in town the village youngman gets not only lured to them but gets addicted to them. This makes him to stay on. Then he makes a home, gets his wife and children and a bigger slum-dwelling is created. The wife also works as a daily wage earner, even the children begin to work as domestic help or as rag-pickers. Some of them even turn into small-time thieves and pick-pockets. Thus goes on the life in the slums.

Those who have stayed on for sometime and had made some money, forget about their village life. They manage an illegal electric connection and there are hundreds and thousands of slum-dwellers who own coloured T.Vs. Where can they get such an entertainment in their rural homes? Those in the villages learn of these achievement and acquisitions and they also get lured to come to town.

How dirty, how unhealthy, how obnoxious is the living in these slums — it can only be known when seen; can hardly be imagined. Most unhealthy living conditions, most unhygienic atmosphere — drains, lanes, dogs and pigs, littered filth — diseases and even deaths on that account — still slums stay on.

This problem is becoming harder to be tackled. It can only be solved when the rural area of the country is improved. More means of employment to the rural population, cottage industries and the proper marketing of their products; electricity reaching the villages; means of entertainment available — then only the attraction of town life can be lessened and population migration from villages to towns be minimised. This situation alone can solve this problem of growing slums.

POINTS TO REMEMBER

- Slums are a growing problem for our country.
- It is the population migration from villages to towns that has led to their creation.
- Our population in the villages and lack of resources to feed the added mouths, make people to migrate in search of jobs.
- No place of shelter in the towns, slum-dwellings are made.
- Political patronage also responsible for their growth as slum-dwellers become vote-banks.
- The added attractions of town life also are reasons for the migration of rural population and for the growth of slums.
- Living conditions in slums — most unhealthy and unhygienic.
- Village life be improved, modern amenities made available; cottage industries started as source of additional income, then only growth of slums can be checked.

❑ ❑ ❑

16. SUPERSTITIONS

Man has kept on believing in some power — unseen but present and working. It is this belief of his which has given rise to superstitions. They are unreasonable and irrational, though but they had been existing and they still exist inspite of all science and scientific development. They exist and are believed in not only in the East but also in the West.

Man began to believe in superstitions when he had a feeling that he was at the mercy of natural elements. Some superstitions also were created due to social values.

Forces of nature had ever been worshipped. Even the Greeks, the Pagans — worshipped elements of nature in the forms of gods and goddesses. There were gods and goddesses among Pagans for every phenomena or force of nature. So has it been with the ancient Indian tradition. The sun, moon, stars, planets, even plants were and continue to be worshipped with the belief that they have the power to influence our lives.

'It is the effect of some evil star' — that is what people say when some disease or disaster overtakes them. This is what even the people of the West have been believing. Shakespeare has made full use of these superstitions in his plays. Ghosts and witches have been made significant characters by Shakespeare in his plays. Calpurnia, the wife of Julius Ceasar, in Shakespeare's play 'Julius Ceasar' sees a dreadful dream which foretells her of some grave tragedy befalling her husband. The horses are said to grow wild and eat one another, before King Duncan is killed by Macbeth in the play Macbeth. Storms blow before tragedy overtakes King Lead in the play by Shakespeare. All these happenings show how people believed in such superstitions.

Even till today the number '13' is treated as an inauspicious number in England; the salt spilling over the dinner table is treated as an ill-omen.

In India, a cat crossing the way while some one departs on a journey or some one sneezing at the time of departure for a journey are treated as ill-omens. The hooting of an owl or the wailing sound of a dog or the long mewing of a cat in the backyard of the house are treated as bad omens; while a pot full of milk or water being carried in front on the onset of a journey is an auspicious thing. Curd offered before the start of a journey or a fish presented before on the doorstep when one leaves on a journey are treated as auspicious signs in India.

Students going to appear at the examinations are still another group in India who are much too susceptible to superstitions. A visit to the temple prior to proceeding for the examination — it is time to turn to religion and beliefs. Candidates turn to a 'taveez-wala' — a lucky stone. A boy going for the examination forgets his pen at home, he would not go back home but preferring borrowing it from his friend candidates — going back home once set out for examination is a bad omen. Even if caught in a traffic jam the candidate would not take the shorter route as the longer route has been auspicious. The stationery to be carried for the examination should be put in the 'puja' room the night before the examination in the morning. The girl had been doing so ever in the past and had secured 'A' grade marks so how could she give that up.

Such are superstitions — they might be considered weird or wild but they are there and no science, no advancement of knowledge perhaps can take these away.

It is, perhaps, a sense of insecurity or just a sense of faith due to past positive or negative experience which sets the mind to keep on believing in superstitions. They may appear irrational but, somehow, they are there — East, West, North, South — that has nothing to do with it — they have been there and they may continue to be there — even the most educated would also go with them and keep them at the back of their minds.

Political leaders are found waiting for the auspicious day or the auspicious hour to file their nominations for elections or take the oath of office.

All this is even at the highest places when science has so far advanced.

There are superstitions which have been created out of some Social Considerations. Sleeping at dusk is treated as a sign that one may fall ill. It is actually that one should not be languid or lazy in the evening. Do not cut the 'Peepal' or the 'Baniyan' tree — that only is a superstition to save trees from destruction. Dogs are very sensitive to natural calamities and become very restless before a natural calamity actually occurs.

These are some of the superstitions which generally people keep believing in the West as well as in the East.

Human mind and human soul keeps on believing that there is some hidden power somewhere which governs their lives and this is the basis of some of these superstitions. The belief in them has gone on, also because some of the superstitions believed in have proved to bring about the anticipated results or effects. May be it is just coincidental but that makes belief in them all the more firm.

There is no logic behind belief in these superstitions but they have grown age-old and even all the scientific advancement of thought does not make them disappear.

But the less we subject ourselves to them the better, otherwise every moment of life would be on tenterhooks.

POINTS TO REMEMBER

- Superstitions and belief in them is only due to the fact that man believes in some power beyond his comprehension which influences his life.
- Forces of nature had even been worshipped both in the West as well as in the East.
- 'Evil stars' — that one says when some tragedy befalls.
- Shakespeare has depicted superstitions in his plays. He also brings Ghosts and witches in his plays.
- There are certain superstitions in which people still behave in the West as well as in the East. Perhaps some coincidence has confirmed the faith in them. Examinees have their own superstitions and examples of their beliefs are numerous and of varied sorts, and they cannot be given up for their own reasons.
- Some Social considerations are also the basis of certain superstitions — don't sleep at dusk, don't harm or cut certain trees.
- Howsomuch science may advance superstitions and belief in them shall continue, though one must not be too much governed by them otherwise every moment of life would be full of anxiety and tension.

❑ ❑ ❑

17. A VISIT TO A ZOO

Zoo is a place where birds, reptiles, animals and beasts are kept in cages. Large area of land is covered for the maintenance of these zoos. People, particularly children find it greatly entertaining to watch these animals and beasts. One cannot go to the forests to see them and even if one goes there all of them cannot be found to be there.

It is a variety of birds, animals and beasts who are kept in a zoo. Rare varieties, even those brought from foreign lands are kept there. In this way the visitors can get a sight of even such animals and beasts which they could never have seen. The lion from Africa, the kangaroo from Australia, the zebra, the polar bear, the chimpanzee, the gorilla, the white tiger, the white peacocks; the parrots of different varieties, the giant crocodiles, the huge pythons — the names are innumerable — all in one zoo. Where can one find to see all these at one place except in a zoo.

Zoos are keeping in tact and looking after such animals and beasts, whose species are being threatened. There are about one thousand species of birds, animals and beasts which are gradually becoming extinct — non-existent. There are various reasons for this. But even these rare varieties are still being kept and looked after in these zoos.

Zoos and their maintenance shows that man has a love for animals, beasts and birds. They are also a part of nature and man cannot ignore them, rather they give people an idea how much variety is there in nature. Visiting a zoo brings men closer to nature, makes men to develop a liking for animals, birds and beasts. They have a geographical importance as well as the visitors by watching the species brought from different lands can get an idea how and where these animals and beasts live — what is the climate and the natural habitat in which they grow.

The maintenance of a zoo is a big exercise. Animals or beasts brought from the country of a particular climate have to be kept in the climate and temperature and surroundings that suit their original habitat. If all that arrangement is not made these animals, beasts and birds cannot survive. A chimpanzee or a gorilla should have tall trees for them to jump around, the lions or tigers should have a pool of water to cool themselves in during hot summers. Then all these animals and beasts and birds and reptiles must be served with the food of their taste and their appetite. A lion or a tiger or a leopard should have the due quantity of raw meat; a monkey, or a gorrilla is a vegetarian and should be fed on that diet. There are animals which should be fed on fishes; the python should have food that it needs — it can devour a whole goat.

So visiting a zoo gives the visitor not only fun but knowledge too — knowledge about so many habits and taste of so many variety of animals, beasts and birds.

A zoo has to maintain its own medical staff too — the veterinary doctor who should be duly qualified and competent. Even, sometimes, surgical operations have to be performed on the animals and beasts.

The visitors, sometimes, cause a great risk to the lives of animals. They throw some eatables in plastic bags and the animals eat them along with the bag, which bag does not get dissolved, rather gets stuck in their intestines causing even their death sometimes. The visitors to the zoos, particularly the children should be duly warned not to feed these animals in this manner otherwise what would be fun for them can become the cause of death for a rare variety of the zoo-inmate.

In this way zoos are a place to teach, to learn, to enjoy — they are the places which brings men in the company of their fellows on this earth — the animals, beasts, birds and so many other creatures. It tells us more and still more about God's creation on this earth. Jesus Christ had said, "Love thy neighbour as thy ownself" to which Mahatma Gandhi added — "Every living being is thy neighbour" "Love all, that is what a zoo teaches".

POINTS TO REMEMBER

- A zoo is a place where the rare variety of birds, beasts, animals and other creatures are kept.
- A zoo is a place which gives to the visitor joy as well as knowledge about nature and nature's varieties of life on this earth.
- Zoo provides a chance to study the zoological as well as geographical conditions of this earth — where under what climate what animals or beasts live.
- A zoo shows man's love for other creatures of this creation and man's care in looking after them — maintenance of a zoo needs great care and caution. Animal life is as important as human life — that is what is learnt.
- Visiting a zoo is a lesson in itself — lesson in the variety of life that is in God's creation.

❑ ❑ ❑

18. SOCIAL SERVICE LEAGUE IN SCHOOL

It was a pleasant and really an appreciable sight to see one day, young boys in school uniform guiding and guarding the traffic on the road crossing which had no redlight. Eager to know how and why they were there doing this risky job, one who was a stand-by pleasantly said, "This is a part of the job that our school social service league has assigned to us for today. 'Remarkable' was my reaction and my curiosity grew more to know more what this 'Social Service League' of the school was. When the duty of the one on the traffic crossing pedestal was over and he stepped down to be replaced by another. I asked the one who had stepped down — 'Oh! wonderful, but let me know what this Social Service League of your school is and what its programme is?'

The boy very pleasantly as if with a sense of achievement told me —

"There is a Social Service League which has been formed by the students of the school themselves under the guidance of two teachers. Saturdays the school keeps a holiday and this is the day allotted for social work. There are in all ten batches of students of the senior classes. They are assigned different Social Service Ventures turn by turn. One batch goes to the slums nearby to teach children who do not go to schools. They play with them and teach them as they play. The children enjoy playing and this makes their learning enjoyable to them. Now the children wait for a Saturday when boys would be there with new games to play and then teach them. During just one month the children have learnt counting upto hundred and writing some alphabets. Gradually they would learn to read and write.

Another batch does the cleaning of the lanes of the slums. Seeing them doing the cleaning with brooms and baskets — the women of the slums come out and have begun to give their helping hand in the process.

The garbage thus collected is deposited in a big pit that existed there and it is covered with earth.

Still another batch goes round telling about sanitation and health problems. They also carry some basic medicines which they have procured through donations from chemists of the area.

There is one batch which plants 'saplings' of trees and puts enclosures around them in the area around the school.

We also plan to go to the neighbouring villages during longer holidays, stay there, share the life of the villagers, show them films on sanitation, on diseases that occur due to bad sanitation, present street plays on social evils like child marriage, untouchability and dowry. We sing and dance and play and the village folk enjoy it and learn from us. Not only that they also have begun singing, dancing and enjoying what we are doing. They are becoming a part of our programme. Once we are able to inspire them we shift to another village and keep revisiting the earlier villages which we had undertaken under our scheme.

We find a lot of change in the ways and views of the village folk and that "gives us so much of satisfaction that our efforts have succeeded".

I felt really overwhelmed with the energy, the enthusiasm and the dedication with which these boys were working. Their Social Service League was doing a really good work.

Schools all over should follow this example and if they really do, the society would be so much benefitted. People would become conscious of the social problems and may begin working themselves in their own localities to carry on the good work. Such a Social Service League of this school is something which sets an example worthy of being followed.

POINTS OF REMEMBER

- Boys were found manning the traffic transactions and controlling traffic — a unique sight.
- Enquiries revealed that they were a part of the Social Service League of their school.
- Every Saturday was off at school and boys of this league took up social work — teaching children in the slums, cleaning the lanes of the slums, telling them about the dangers of bad sanitation; distributed medicines, planting 'saplings' and protecting them.
- The boys of this league even visited neighbouring villages during longer holidays and stayed there. Through film shows, street plays made the village folk learn lessons about social evils — child marriages, untouchability, dowry etc. and making the village folk part of their programmes — a worthy activity.
- All schools should follow this example. The society would stand to benefit a lot if this happens.

❑ ❑ ❑

19. SMOKING AND DRUGS — A MENACE TO LIFE

We find youngmen feel big, as if, puffing a cigarette and throwing out smoke at the company in which they are. They begin the game out of fun and curiosity how it tastes; then the game takes the shape of a showmanship and in due course of time they find that they have got addicted to smoking and cannot give it up. It sometimes, begins with just a few cigarettes a day, then it becomes a few packets a day and some turn into chain smokers — one out, the other is lighted.

Cigarettes contain nicotine, along with tobacco and it is this nicotine which makes one addicted to smoking. It has an intoxicating effect and once a man's nerves catch this intoxication, the nerves keep on needing it and one feels lethargic and dull without a puff because the nerves are constantly asking for the kick. This is addiction, which once caught on becomes life long and cannot be given up. There have been people who have gone to sleep smoking and have got their quilt and bedding burnt — and it is then they get awakened. There have been and are writers and authors whose pen would move only when they are puffing out. Without that puff their mind, as if goes to rest and would not work. Young and old — a habit is a habit with anybody and a habit once formed is hard to be given up.

Nicotine is an element which slowly and gradually passes on and gets deposited in the nerves and in the lungs. This gradual deposition causes lung diseases — bronchitis, bronchial asthma, tuberculosis and even cancer — of which there is no cure. Smoking thus can be life-taking. People know it, still they go on with it. Smokers even can have their arteries blocked with nicotine which can cause a heart attack. It is for all these fatal results that it has become compulsory for the cigarette manufacturing companies to print a warning on every pocket — 'Smoking is dangerous for health'. Inspite of the warning forced upon to be issued by the manufacturers themselves, the consumers keep consuming the danger even at the risk of their lives. And cigarettes continue to be manufactured, stocked and sold the world over.

It is not only the smoker who sustains the harm; even those who are not smoking but are in the company of smokers are also harmed. They have to inhale the smoke emitted out by their friends in company. It is, therefore, that smoking has been banned in cinema halls or in conference halls. In foreign countries outside India, there are smoking chambers attached to big offices — those who cannot do without smoking have to go to those chambers to have a smoke — smoking in the office room is not permitted.

Those who do not smoke find the smoke of a cigarette, intolerable — their head begins to ache if someone is puffing out the smoke around them.

This is, thus, a great menace to health and the upcoming, growing youngmen must understand the risks involved. They can, well in time, learn the lesson and let them not allow themselves to fall a prey to this 'disease' — it is really a 'disease' which once it catches can aggravate into any proportion.

Life is a gift given by God, let us live it well, let us live it healthily and health is happiness.

Grimmer still is another still greater a menace than smoking a cigarette. It is the addiction to drugs which is fast catching up with the young. Everyday there are reports in the newspapers how the racket of drug-traffickers are caught. One or two kgs. of heroin goes into crores of rupees in money value. It is a bye-product of opium and Afghanistan used to be a big opium growing country. There are international gangs operating in drug-trafficing as it gives ready and big money.

The addiction to drugs is also a growing menace. One who gets addicted to it cannot do without it; gets badly upset if he does not get his dose and do anything to have the kicking dose. People addicted to drugs have been found to be selling out everything to fulfil their urge — without their dose they lie listless and lost. Morphine is still another drug which the addicts inject in their veins. There are outlets where such drugs are available by the backdoor. The addicts know their supplier. Even the cold drink parlours or the betel-shops in the dark alleys are dealing in these drugs. Once got into the habit and the addiction, no inhibitions, no restraints can stop the addict. Youngmen easily fall a prey to such menaces, knowing not that they are risking their health and running their lives. Hostels of educational institutions get to become centres of this menace. Youngmen and even young women — neglected or not properly looked after by parents are easy targets of this disease. They suffer a neglect at home, so they seek company outside and the drug dealers are ready to catch them quick. Once caught, they become a part of the racket. They lose the joy of life in seeking this false 'Kick' — lose money, lose health — pilfer money from home or seek it by unlawful means. They must have their 'dose' at any cost.

This is how smoking and drugs — beware of it — that is the warning to the young — if they want to achieve anything in life. Without achievement life is hardly worth living — this the young must known.

POINTS TO REMEMBER

- Smoking grows, first into a show and a fashion then a habit.
- The content of a cigarette is nicotine which causes addiction and this slowly and gradually gets deposited in the veins, the lungs — causes lung and heart diseases.
- 'Smoking is dangerous for health' is inscribed on every packet of cigarette — law demands this inscription.
- Those who do not themselves smoke but are in a smoker's company also inhale the smoke and suffer from its dangers.
- Youngmen must get warned against this menace if they want to live a healthy and happy life.
- Drugs are also a greater menace. Heroin, morphine and such other drugs once caught on shall ever be an addiction.
- People addicted to drugs can sell away everything to get their dose for a 'Kick' without which they would be listless and lost.
- Youngmen and women must be cautions of this menace — life is meant for achievements without achievement all life is lost and addiction to drugs would cause a derailment of life.

❏ ❏ ❏

20. THE SCHOOL LIBRARY

Library is the heart and soul of an educational institution. Books are the treasure from which as much as is drawn the more the drawer gains and that treasure never gets exhausted. A well equipped library — equipped with the best selected books, magazines and newspapers should form an integral part of the schooling of children. Children need to be told, they need to be encouraged in the use of the library and teachers have constantly to keep a watch on what the child reads, what he learns and how much does he assimilate from these books. A separate period for every class needs to be provided in the school timetable in which children should be required to go to the library, read books and magazines and take down notes of what they read. These notes, thereafter, need to be checked by teachers. This would give to the teachers an idea what the child most prefers to know about and how he reacts to what he reads. It would be an automatic psychological estimation of the child — the way that his personality is moulding; what his interests are and what he plans to become. What he is learning; what he takes interest in, would get reflected in the choice of books or magazines and teachers would get to know the mould and manner of his thinking and working of his mind.

The school library, in order to fulfil its purposefulness should have books for all ages and for all minds and the librarian, incharge of the library should himself or herself be knowledgable as to be able to recommend what books to be chosen on what subject.

Further more, the school library should have a nice, spacious seating arrangement in every way to draw students to it.

Students, during assemblies, should be informed about the utility and usefulness of books and need to be told how books could be their best companions. Books could give them what no other companion can give — other companions could quarrel with them; push them and hurt them sometimes; companions can change their attitudes and behaviour but whatever is contained in the books shall ever remain constant and the same for ages after ages. The word once printed in a book shall ever be the same for all times and keep on giving the same message generation after generation.

Milton, a great English poet had said — 'A good book is the precious life-blood of a master spirit, treasured and embalmed in its pages for ages after ages'. Great thoughts, great ideals, great pieces of information — deep and varied — are provided through books and a library is the treasure house of such thoughts, ideals and information. A school would be failing in its purpose if it does not have in it a library — well housed, well equipped, well staffed and well-furnished.

POINTS TO REMEMBER

- Library is the heart and soul of an educational institution.
- Children should be encouraged to use the library which should be properly furnished and properly equipped with good books.
- There should be books for all ages and for all tastes.
- The librarian should know all about the books and should be able to guide students in choosing good books.
- Books are the best companions—they never quarrel; they never change. They are a treasure house of knowledge.

❑❑❑

21. IMPORTANCE OF GAMES AND SPORTS IN EDUCATION

Education does not only mean what is taught in a class room. It is a process of learning and lessons can be learnt from all aspects of life. Enlightenment of the mind is the purpose of total education. Building up of the personality and character of a young boy or girl is what is intended by education. A classroom education enlightens the mind with new thoughts and fresh perceptions given in the books and explained and elucidated by the teacher.

The play field has many other lessons to give and to be learnt. The performance of a team game depends upon the cooperation and the joint, concerted effort of all the players. If any of the links is weak or is not performing as well as it should the total effort fails. In the game of football, hockey, rugby or basketball the central forward of the team can only score a goal if the left and right wings give him the right support — a proper and timely pass. If the one on the defence position fails to check the advancing forward player of the opposite team the chances of scoring of a goal brighten up. Many goals are saved by the alertness, agility and fore sight of the goal keeper. Similarly, in the game of cricket, the bowler, the fielders each one has a very crucial part to play and it is on his performance that the result of the match would depend. The batsman needs to have the due concentration and the ability to strike or deflect the ball in the right proper manner and direction. This is all about the team games.

In such games as tennis or badminton or squash or chess, in a singles match, the total concentration of the player's mind and his ability to cash on the weak points of his opponent alone can make him to win. In field sports — the races, the hurdles, swimming, and in the event of throws, the full use of one's alertness and agility and the full use of one's power puts him or her at the top of the victory stand.

So what does all this mean. Games and Sports train a player or a sportsman to keep himself fully fit in body and mind. To do well in a team event the spirit to cooperate and to conjoin efforts gives the mind a training in the art of cooperation, adjustment and accord. That is why they are called 'Team Games'. It is not one but all who have to coordinate to gain a win. This team spirit learnt on the play field teach them the value of mutual trust, mutual goodwill and mutual help — lessons learnt on the field are lessons learnt for life — in life's every field and every venture. Jointly man can work wonders; a joint effort is the keynote to success.

Individual events give the mind a training in concentration and determination to win — these two lessons if followed in life, can bring success in any field.

Thus games and sports have lessons to teach, have thought to be valued and worked upon — they educate the mind in their own way for success in life. They are equally as important as what we learn in a classroom.

POINTS TO REMEMBER

- Education does not mean only classroom teaching.
- Total education is the total development of the student's personality — his body as much as his mind.
- The play field helps to develop the body.
- Games — particularly team games — teach the leasson of combination, joint effort and team spirit — which lessons are great lessons to be learnt.
- Individual games teach concentration, total attention and agile activity.
- All these trainings and lessons learnt on the play field are lessons learnt for life — that is the importance of Games and Sports.

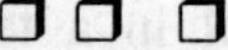

22. EXTRA CURRICULAR ACTIVITIES EDUCATE MORE THAN CLASSROOM TEACHING

An ideal school gives to students the scope and the spirit of healthy competition — to excel at all levels. Class work and the home work given by teachers have their academic importance; in this also one who excels wins the praise and appreciation from the teachers. But academic distinctions alone do not fulfill all the purpose for which the school exists. A school is the work shop of life-building in which the raw material is the nascent mind of young pupils. The principal, the teachers are the moulders of this raw material into the ideal mould. For this process many more activities, other than the class-room ones, are needed to fulfill the purpose. A young pupil might have the potential and the natural talent to excel in games and sports and he needs to go to play field and the sports ground for the purpose.

There can be students whose natural bent of mind is towards creative art and the art room is his field where he needs to be given the chance to exhibit his potential. Even little children of the nursery or the primary classes can draw such lines and make such figures which may amaze an on-looker and may be led to exclaim — 'What an idea, how could he imagine this?' One cannot and does not know how much talent in what direction lies in a child's brain. This can only come out when he or she is given that opportunity. The school has to provide such chances and explore out the pearls from the sea-depths of the young mind. Art competitions of different level of students are activities that need to be arranged and the excellence in that to be rewarded and encouraged.

There are boys and girls who have a knack of oration. They have in them an amount of self-confidence that they can face spectators and audience. Elocution contests and debates offer them the chance to exhibit this latent talent of theirs. Such inter-class or inter-school competitions should regularly be held which would further them to become good debators — who knows, they may one day become parliamentarians and what they have gained during their school days may place them in good stead in that field.

Cultural shows, dramatics performances and mono-actings are events which schools generally hold and it is so necessary for schools to hold them. That is also a part of total education. Taking part in such events gives children a sense of self-confidence and embellishes their accomplishments which they possess or can even develop. Anything, any activity which helps in the development of the total personality of young boy or girl is a part of education and competitions, the effort to excel from others, is an incentive which must be provided to a young mind. Such an opportunity is offered to them only through such cultural and extra curricular activities. Opening up of personality, developing the latent talents; promotion of the intellectual effort and an opportunity of healthy competition — all these are factors which an educational institution should always encourage — only when it does this, it fulfills its role in the total education of the young.

POINTS TO REMEMBER

- Class work and home work have their academic importance.
- The school is a workshop in which the raw material — the young students' mind is to be moulded in the over all proportionate mould.
- There can be students whose mind is more bent towards creative art-drawing, painting or music.
- The school is to search out the pearl from the ocean depth of the mind and give it a shape and the design.
- Extra curricular activities of all forms — debates, elocution contests, quiz contests, dramatic performances painting competitions — make up for the total education.

23. STUDENTS — THEIR ROLE IN THE INDIA OF TODAY

Students, particularly those who have crossed the teenage, can render great service to the country. The country badly needs their services but it is they who have to understand this. They have reached an age when energy bubbles in them, maturity has begun to dawn upon their minds; they have the capability to think and discriminate the right from the wrong. They are in such a large multitude — they are like a surging wave of a turbulent river which, if properly controlled and channelized can render the vast tracts of land green; but if left uncontrolled can work havoc and devastation. They have to know their potentiality of gainful service to the nation — but as today, they do not seem to know it or they do not want to know it. They shirk that responsibility which they should themselves offer to shoulder. That is the sorry state of affairs. Their energies get wasted in wrongful pursuits, in organizing strikes and 'Bands', in putting forth demands which do not concern them or could get solved by sitting and talking it out across the table. But soon they form a 'mob' and a mob has no mind of its own. It is led by frenzy and grows fanatic. Reason and good sense never appeals to a mob. This is the scenario all the country over while problems frown on us or like cankers are ready to eat into the vitals of our body politic.

Therefore it is that students have to learn the lesson the right way that they are to be the rightful citizens of tomorrow; they are to be the torch bearers; are to be the harbingers of the new age; the new century that is knocking at our door. They can make history or mar it.

What are they to do? — let them be told.

India has a rural base and most of our students come from that background. They know full well the problems that face the people in the rural sector. The most important of it all is illiteracy. Students have long holidays at their disposal. During these periods they can organize themselves into groups and take upon themselves the task of each one of them making five illiterate persons literate in their area. All over the country if students take up this challenge and meet it, what a tremendous service at a vast scale would they render.

Religious tolerance, and breaking the barriers of castes is still another greater social good that they can render. They can do it through words as well through deeds. While in their villages during holidays they may organize meetings, they may arrange mass dinners, they may usher in a new awakening. At the outset they can face staunch opposition from their own elders in this task but slowly and gradually they can persuade cajole and convince them — the elders — into accepting that temples are meant for all; that all religions lead to the same goal; that the nation is more important than the caste, community and religion. They can give examples and prove their point that soldiers fighting on the fronts to protect the country — all live together, dine together, they know no discrimination but fight for the common cause of saving the country's honour. Their common aim and a common goal makes them one.

Students, during their vacations can also launch sanitation drives in their villages; clean the drains and fill up the puddles; give the village a cleaner took — once they have done it, villagers would feel encouraged and inspired to keep up the task.

Students can even form a group to stage some corner plays against the social evils such a dowry or discrimination against the girl child. What may not be taught through words can be taught through performance — education through entertainment is the best way to teach. Preach as you play — that is the best way of teaching the ignorant.

Planting of trees and awakening the conscience of the village folk regarding the environmental pollution is one big task that students can perform. Let them propagate the plan of one man or woman 'one tree' or one child in the village school 'one tree' — what a tremendous afforestation drive can this effort bring about. Let each one planting a sapling or seedling give it his name and let the tree be known by that name — it would be fun and fame but a great national service.

Those students who belong to the towns can carry out sanitation drives in their localities; hold free medical camps with the help of their friends among the doctors, hold 'nukkad nataks' to educate the people on social problems, carry out the literacy drive through night schools.

But all this can be done only if students realize their potential and have in them an urge and a zeal towards service of the country.

POINTS TO REMEMBER

- Students, at least those who have crossed their teenage can render a great service to the country.
- Such a large multitude of youngman is like a surging torrent which can be channelized in formative channels. Their energies should not go waste in unfruitful 'Bandhs' and 'Strikes'.
- Students are to be the citizens of the nation of tomorrow and should play the part of nation building.
- What should students do to serve the nation?

(a) Remove illiteracy by arranging camps during holidays in the villages or the urban 'bastis' and try to make at least five illiterates literate — five to one — as the ratio.

(b) Give lessons in religious and communal tolerance — arrange mass dinners.

(c) Launch sanitation drives — clean the lanes and drains and inspire the village folk or the 'basti' folk to take up the drive.

(d) Stage corner shows against social evils like dowry or lavish expenditure in marriage etc. or population control.

(e) Planting trees — 'one student one tree' — 'to spread this message among students.

But to carry out all these projects students have first to develop a sense of nationalism and patriotism.

❑❑❑

24. SCIENCE IS A GOOD SLAVE BUT A BAD MASTER

We today revel in the idea that we are living in a world of science and science can work wonders for us. True it is that science has revolutionized modern life. What our forefathers, half a century ago, could not even dream of, we have that at our beck and call. Electricity is a wonder and what it is doing would have appeared to be a fairy tale for our forefathers. A button is pressed the room gets flooded with light, the fan moves, the A.C. cools or warms the room, water is boiled or cooled even is frozen, eatables can be preserved for days.

Human suffering has greatly been eliminated. Science has investigated into diseases and found startling cures for them. Artificial limbs can be fitted to the disabled bodies, even kidneys and heart are being transplanted. Painless operations are being performed.

Machinery has eliminated human labour and made life more mechanical and less arduous. Means of communication — The Fax, The E-mail, The cordless telephones are really wonderful means given to us by Science. The atomic energy if put to use for peaceful purposes can work wonders.

We have begun to feel that life without the modern scientific gadgets is impossible.

True, that all this has happened and we feel beholden to science and the scientists. But there is the other side of the picture too.

Man has become a slave to the machines. Human labour has been minimized but that has led to a more luxurious living and less of physical activity. Mankind has begun suffering from such ailments which our hard-working forefather never knew of. More and more use of machines had led to large scale unemployment. The pesticides and germicides used in saving the crops are sending out such alarming signals as demolishing and dismantling the ozone layer which was protecting the earth from the evil effects of the sun rays. The world is getting exposed to the situation of great alarm and danger.

The atomic energy is being used for destructive purposes and the nuclear explosions are causing radiations which are fatal for mankind. Can we ever forget what happened to Nagasaki and Hiroshima in Japan during the II World War? Do we want to live under such further threats of large scale devastation and destruction?

The worst that science has done is the demolition of our faith in the Divine Power. The Darwanian Theory of evolution has given a death blow to our faith that there is some Creator — the super power — far too superior which has created this universe and good or bad actions invite rewards or punishments to us in the form of Heaven and Hell. The scientists of today consider themselves as masters of nature. Inspite of all scientific advancements, earthquakes still occur, cyclones still come and leave back large-scale loss of life and properties. If man has become the master of nature why cannot he avoid such disasters. So this proves what Shakespeare had said 'There're more things in heaven and earth which are beyond our philosophies'.

Therefore, what is necessary is that we may use science as our slave — take the utmost advantage from it but should not permit it to become our master. We have to keep the 'genie' under our control, use it for the good of mankind; cure diseases with its help, explore treasures of this earth through it; communicate with one another at the quickest pace but keep its dangerous use under check. Let science remain our 'slave' and not allow it to become our master. Let science like Aladdin's 'genie' remain in Alladin's controlling power not to overpower him, and be a menace to mankind.

POINTS TO REMEMBER

- We feel happy to think that we are living in a world of science and its wonders.
- We have really been provided with lots of comforts in our homes by electricity.
- In the field of medicine and surgery, great advancement has been made and so it is in the field of industry and communication.

  All these are the advantages which science has given to us.
- But the disadvantages are also there.
- Elimination of human labour has made men to suffer from various diseases.
- The use of pesticides and germicides are affecting the atmosphere and depleting the ozone layer which is dangerous.
- The atomic energy has been used for destructive purposes.

- The Darwanian Theory of Evolution has shaken man's faith in God, who has been treated as the creator and benefactor of mankind.
- Let Science be the slave of man and not be allowed to become its master.

❑ ❑ ❑

25. TELEVISION — THE GOOD AND THE BAD ABOUT IT

Television has become more or less a craze of the modern society and a coloured T.V. set is regarded a status symbol. This has more or less, replaced the radio, of which, earlier it had started as only a link. Now this attached limb has become the body throwing the sponsorer in the background.

Television can play a great part in educating and instructing people in the right way of life which it is trying to do. Entertainment is its major part as to see the visual appearance of the performers on the screen adds more attraction. In the radio one could only hear the voice but in T.V. there is the voice as well as the person speaking or singing or dancing or performing. That is a great advantage of a T.V. production, and that is why it has taken a march ahead of all other forms. People can watch even a full picture in a T.V., hence it is that so many cinema houses had to close down their shop.

With so much of attraction added to the T.V., it should be seen to that along with the entertainment that T.V. provides to its viewers greater emphasis should be laid on its educational aspect in which field it can play a great part. Especially in a country like India, where the majority of population is illiterate, T.V. can play a very significant role. And it is trying to live up to this expectation. Lessons for school going students particularly on subjects like science and mathematics; in geography and history — even in English are being televised and they are proving greatly beneficial to the young students. Important events of history are being projected on the T.V. screen giving to the spectators a visual view of what had happened. Even some of the serials — like Ramayana, Mahabharata, Srikrishna and many other such serials based on religious mythology have been produced after great research and have enlightened even the educated mind on many of those details of these mythological stories that they did not know about. Similarly serials on Tipu or on the freedom struggle of our country have highlighted many forgotten or unknown details to students of history. Talks, discussions and interviews by and of great scholars, politicians and leaders give us, sitting at home, the inside of many events and many views. The Krishi Darshan programme educates the farmer of our land. The Discovery channel or the National Geographical channel have such vivid and lively details to give about the animal life, the beast life; even about lands and people which we can never see, visit or meet.

Similarly, games and sports have gained so much popularity through T.V. visuals. Sitting within our homes we can watch the Cricket World Series, the Wimbledon Tennis, or the World Olympic events.

All these are — the all good about the T.V.

But then there are some — the bad — about this as well.

T.V. has gained such a passion for the young children in particular, that they neglect studies and playing games and participating in sports has become a far cry. Those games fields which used to be buzzing with activity after the regular teaching hours in schools and colleges, lie deserted. In most of the educational institutions games and sports have been given a go-bye and this is one of the reasons why this vast country of ours is not able to produce world class athletes and players. There may be other causes for this too but T.V. shows taking away all the time and attention of our youngsters is also one such cause.

Coloured T.V. has been found to have a baneful effect on the health of the viewers. It has a polluting influence. The rays emanating from them cause diseases of the eye as well as of the body.

Television, thus should be treated only as a slave and should not be tolerated to become the master of minds of the young and old alike.

POINTS TO REMEMBER

- Television has become a craze in the world of today.
- Television can play a great part in imparting education.
- Lessons in science, mathematics, geography, history, our mythology can be imparted through television.
- But at present T.V. is concentrating more on entertainment which keeps the young glued to the T.V. distracting them from their studies and games.
- Long hours of watching coloured T.V. can affect the eye sight as well as can affect the body.
- Restrictive use of T.V. is advisable.

26. OUR VILLAGE LIFE — HOW TO IMPROVE IT

Even though the big towns and the metropolises are facing the great problem of the migration of the population to these towns, still India lives in the villages. 80% population of the country lives in the villages.

But with all the development schemes launched and being launched for the improvement and development of the village life, the life therein remains still backward, where much still remains to be done, much to be desired. In several parts of the country even the basic needs are not available. Clean drinking water, proper shelter and sanitation, proper health care — all these are crying needs of India's rural areas. India is a vast country and inspite of large scale projects launched from time to time to better the looks and life of our rural folk, much still remains to be desired.

It was as far back as in 1952 that the community development programme was launched. Under this programme was planned the supply of improved seeds, modern implements and chemical manures to the farmers — most of the rural population are agriculturists — minor irrigation projects were started, facilities to improve the breed and looking after of the live-stocks was taken up, some village industries were also pushed up.

The 'integrated rural development programme' intended to provide employment to the rural population. Big irrigation projects, construction of huge dams had been taken up to supply to our farmers timely water for their crops, electricity to their tube wells.

A rural health programme was launched in the year 1977 and by 1982-83 it was expected to cover the entire rural population under this scheme. Community health workers were trained and are being trained to render the barely necessary and immediate medical aid.

Employment facilities to the rural population were also envisaged to be provided — the target was fixed at by the year 1987. But there still remains much to be desired, much to be achieved. For the benefit of the milk producers of the rural population a scheme called 'Operation Flood' was launched; the plan behind this programme was to establish a direct link between the rural milk producers with the processing units established in the urban areas. Along with this had been launched the scheme of improving the quality of milch cattle by the method of artificial insemination. Such centres for artificial insemination were established at every block level.

Universalization of education for rural children and literacy to the adults have also been schemes launched but not the expected head way could be made in this direction.

Of course, the 'Panchayati Raj' system has been introduced in almost all the states of the country. This is a decentralization policy to make the democratic process to reach the grass roots and make the rural population the dispensers of justice at their own level in all possible ways. It has caught up with the rural folk though much still requires to make this system free from discriminations and discussions.

What is intended and needed is that the rural masses should have a better living, more health facilities, more economic gains for their products, more prosperity, more education, more employment. The commodities that they produce should give them enough gains and exploitation by the middle man may be eliminated. More roads, better transport facilities and greater communication level for this majority population — are dreams of the rural development programmes planned and envisaged. Much has been achieved but still much more is required to be done. Fifty years of independence but only about fifty percent of the achievement targets — this presents a grim picture. Villages and villagers have to be freed from age-old superstitions and raised up to a respectable level. Economic independence and education — these are the basics which alone can do what is intended and planned.

POINTS TO REMEMBER

- India is facing a gigantic problem of the migration of the rural population to the towns.
- The cause of this is that the rural life, the villages have not witnessed that improvement and development inspite of all development schemes launched since, as far back as 1952.
- There have hardly been any facilities of irrigation, availability of electricity, fertilizers, seeds, care of the livestock, employment, rural health education and transport.
- The Panchayat Raj System plans to decentralize the system and place most of the schemes in the hands of the Panchayats.
- Economic independence and education are the prime needs for a better village life.

27. THE PICTURE OF AN IDEAL INDIAN VILLAGE

There is absolutely no harm in at least dreaming the best — at least in thinking what the ideal shape of things can be. To picture an ideal village can be one such dream, which if ever realized would turn our country as model for the other developing countries.

The village is the last and the lowest rung of the ladder of our social set up. Majority of our population lives in the villages and let us plan what an ideal village could be.

To begin with, an ideal village should be one which can easily be reached. Link roads — durable and well constructed—should connect this village with the main highway. This would enable the villages to have an easy access to the towns and the town markets. Trucks and tractor-trolleys could then move to and from the village and the economic life of the village folk would vastly improve only by this one factor. On this one basic improvement depends the entire life of the rural folk.

When economy would improve people of the village can voluntarily feel the need to have a school for children. The government agencies would come to their help in funding a properly built school at least upto the higher secondary level and teachers, who at present shudder to go the inaccessible villages, would easily and readily go and teach in such a school. Education is the basic of all enlightenment. Economy having improved and children provided with education — this would lay the foundation of an enlightened future society. Agriculture — the main source of the rural income will have all the resources ready at hand — fertilizers, seeds of the best variety and pesticides — and then the experts in this field could easily reach them to give the right proper advice in their proper and timely use.

Electricity is still another need for an ideal village — it would help in the working of the tubewells, lighting the lanes and homes and make life more comfortable in every way.

The 'panchayats' would be the nucleus of active constructive working of the villager's welfare. Members of these 'panchayats' would encourage the village folk in general to keep lanes in proper shape and the drains along with them properly cleaned. There would be soak-pits and manure-pits dug up to absorb the drain effluents and the home refuge to convert them into healthy manures.

From animal dung, bio-gas power plants could be built up which could supply gas as well as electricity to the houses and relieve the women folk from the dangers of smoke-caused diseases. Every home will have the gas-supply and that would make life so free from pollution and pollution-caused inhygiene. The village would present such a pleasant and healthy look, offer so much of employment to villagers that they would not think of migrating to the towns in search of employment.

The 'Panchayat Ghar' could be converted into a community centre where a television set could be put up and after the day's work the rural folk could congregate to enjoy shows as well as to hear to talks and discourses on the latest techniques in improving agriculture. They can also watch movies and serials and listen to national and international news.

Village industries would get set up, village markets would begin to be held; implements of daily use could be manufactured and repaired, tractors could be repaired and overhauled. Running to the towns for getting little petty jobs done — would be avoided — the service would be there at their door steps.

This is what an ideal village would be and could be. What is needed is to infuse a new spirit and present a new vision to the village folk. They would work it out; they have the energy — it only needs to be channelized in the right direction. Let first a model village be so formed — others would feel inspired to follow suit. That would really be a great day for our motherland.

POINTS TO REMEMBER

- We, at least, should dream and plan the best — no harm in doing so.
- What should an ideal village have?
  - (a) Link roads connecting the village to the highway — such a road on which trucks and tractor trolleys can move.
  - (b) A school for children at least from the primary to the higher secondary level.
  - (c) Availability of the best seeds and fertilizers and pesticides at low cost.
  - (d) Electricity — to help working the tubewells and canals.
  - (e) Panchayats to really work for the welfare of the village — proper sanitation — clean lanes and clean drains, manure pits and soak pits.
  - (f) Biogas to provide gas to the kitchens and lights in the streets.

(g) Village industries and facilities for the marketing of their products.

(h) Workshops for the repair of tractors and trolleys.

All these, if made available, the village would turn an ideal habitable place.

❑ ❑ ❑

28. GARDENING AS A HOBBY

A hobby is one's best past time. It is something which while giving satisfaction is enjoyable too. But given a choice, gardening is a very pleasant and rewarding as a hobby. A little piece of land in front or at the back or around the house is enough to launch this hobby. After the day's hard work, or even before the day begins — early in the morning and then for the whole day on a holiday one can enjoy to indulge and involve himself in this hobby.

Right from digging the earth, beating down the moulds into fine-soil, then turning them into small beds, mixing the manure in the soil, one is ready to plant the seeds or the saplings or the seedlings and then softly watering them. In the process one has to select what grows where — to give a real glorious glow to the piece of land which may be a pleasure to the eye as also productive for the hobbyists.

If the piece of land is big enough, one arranges and selects proper places for the fruit plants, the papaya, the lemon, the guava, the big banana or even the pomegranate and lichi, but in case it is just a small piece of land one limits oneself to the flowers and a few creepers.

Each day is a day of care and caution, with an eager and an expectant eye one watches the sprouting from the seeds, or the saplings or seedlings, taking roots, and standing up on their own. Gradually the flower seeds have shown up the sproutings and the seedlings showing up new leaves and the growth is watched with such a sense of satisfaction and enjoyment when finally the flowers bloom into their dazzling multi-coloured hues and there is, as if a riot of colours all around. 'Dancing with the daffodils' — this is what the great nature-poet Wordsworth has said and rightly so. The hobbyist's heart also gets elated to watch the perfect result of his labours. And then after months of looking after the grape wine or the papaya or the guava or the banana in a bunch, show up their face first; it is a gratification indeed. The labour has been rewarded.

Thus goes on the game of gardening.

Gardening, as a hobby has so many advantages. One can spend one's leisure time in physical work, which exercises the body; the results elate the mind and the fruits — fresh and free — are a pleasure to be tasted. Spending spare time in useless gossip or straining the eyesight viewing the T.V. — all this is hardly a useful utilization of one's leisure. You dig, you till, you soil with your hands, you even sweat in the process and the least of it all, you are constantly in the company of nature which company is never boring never tiring rather, it is ever rewarding in every way. You reap the fruits of your labour — what else can be so satisfying than that. You are face to face with the spirituality of the matter — how from such a small seed gets produced such beauty, such lustre and such a result. God's nature is wonderful —

that's what you have at last to feel and say. This is thus the most rewarding hobby, if one develops it and enjoys it too.

The hobby of gardening can give us an insight in understanding the purport of what Wordsworth has said in these lines about nature.

One impulse from the vernal wood
May teach you more of man
Of moral evil and of good
Than all the Sages can.

Nature is the book from which one can learn all that the creation is about, the mysteries of life, the beauties of life and the bounties bestowed upon us by the creator.

POINTS TO REMEMBER

- One needs to have a past time and to engage oneself in a hobby of one's choice is the best past time.
- Gardening is a very pleasant and rewarding a hobby.
- It provides scope for physical exercise as well as a mental satisfaction.
- From sowing a seed to the growing of the plant and its fruition are all a very pleasant experience.
- Fresh fruits and vegetables shall be available at one's doorstep. A sense of fulfilment and achievement.
- Last but not the least — a communication with the Divine — the wonder how a plant can grow out of a small seed — a miracle worthy of being watched and thought upon.

❑ ❑ ❑

29. AN INDIAN FESTIVAL

India is a country where in every season, in every part of the year around and in every part of the country one or the other fair or festival is being held. But for the holding of a fair or a festival there is a fair season or a proper occasion assigned to it. Then there is also a seasonal value of such a festival.

Deepawali is one such festival which has a symbolic as well as a rational and a recreational value.

The rainy season is at its wane. The slushy drains and lanes are drying up; the humidity and heat of the weather is gradually subsiding and the temperate shiver in the cool breeze begins to give us an indication of the advent of winter. India is the only country where there are marked seasons that keep changing at the appointed time of the year. After the blistering heat of the summers April, May and June and with the advent of July clouds begin hovering in the sky and the rainy season gives us a much needed relief. The parched earth thirsting for a shower gets the much awaited down pour — there is flooding of rivers and the rivulets, the grass grows green, the trees, and bushes wear a washed look. That is the rainy season which gradually subsides to usher the other season — the winter — in the month of October and November. And it is only so welcome when this refreshing cool shiver of the wintry breeze marks the advent of the festival of Deepawali — the festival of the row of lights. This is a festival which comes fifteen days after the Vijay Dashmi — The day of the conquest of Ravana — the Demon king by Ram. Hence it has got associated with the celebration of this victory — symbolized also as the victory of the Good over the Evil.

Among all the Indian festivals Deepawali or Diwali as it is commonly called is a festival of great festivity. Prior to the advent of the day of this festival houses are cleaned; every nook and corner of the house is supposed to be got rid of all the dust and dirt; the walls are whitewashed or painted and floors are washed and cleaned. It is in this manner that the entire house is disinfected; necessary as it is after the soggy, slushy rainy season which gives rise to insects and germs particularly in the nooks and corners of the house. This is actually an annual cleaning activity of the house and its surroundings; a necessary activity for a healthy living.

Associated as all this is with the celebration of the victory of Ram over Ravana and Ram's arrival after it to Ayodhya, the ritual and the revelry has its social and hygienic value. That is how every such festival in our country has been so planned to get associated with life and living.

The festival is celebrated by lighting lamps in a row over the house tops; over all the wall tops and parapets of the house. Originally these used to be the earthen lamps filled with mustard oil and a wick dipped in the oil. These while illuminating the houses presenting a festive look also attracted worms and insects which had grown in large numbers during the rainy season and which got self immolated, in this manner striking a natural balance in the eco-system.

This is a festival when Hindus worship Lord Ganesh — the God of Commonweal and Goddess Lakshmi — the Goddess of wealth and prosperity. It is actually in this part of the season that the previous crops had been harvested and thrashed and stored and the fresh seeds of a fresh crop are sown in the fields. India has been an agricultural country where crops have ever been the source of wealth and prosperity and of common weal. Thus this worship of Lord Ganesh and Goddess Lakshmi has also its very symbolic significance.

This festival got associated with children enjoying the most with lighting the crackers and such other items of illumination and fun. This had sometimes led to burns and accidents of a serious nature and also have caused a lot of environmental pollution. This year, particularly in Delhi, children launched a 'no-crackers' drive and this was a very welcome feature of environmental consciousness on their part. They could give up fun and frolick to keep the environment free from pollution — really a great move on their part. If children can be taught lessons in consciousness on social issues in this manner and are inspired and invoked to take up other social issues which besmear our social psyche, India can hope for a brighter day though it may result in a less brighter Deepawali for them. Let them learn the lessons of sacrifice for a social cause — a great lesson, indeed, to learn.

So, Deepawali — the 'awali' — or row of 'Deep' — the lamp is a great festival; one of the most festive, one so full of light and glow and at the same time so full of symbolism and so good for the social well being of the people at large.

POINTS TO REMEMBER

- In India, there is, in every season, a fair or a festival. Association with a season has its signficance.
- After the rainy season causing all slush, mud and filth; also insects and germs comes the festivals of Diwali or Deepawali; fifteen days after Vijay Dashami or Dusshehra.

- Diwali enjoins upon all to clean their houses, its every nook and corner and paint or whitewash the walls — all this a ritual but hygienic, after all that dirt of the rainy season.
- Diwali also symbolizes Ram's victory over Ravana — the Good over the Evil.
- The lighting of lamps attracts the insects who get naturally immolated, thus the balance in nature is maintained.
- On this festival people worship Ganesh, the God of Commonweal and Lakshmi, the goddess of wealth and prosperity.

  This is actually celebration of the old harvest stored and the new crop to be sowed — prosperity to Indian masses comes through agriculture.
- Children play with crackers and other items of illumination. But this causes pollution. This year in Delhi, children decided upon 'no crackers' to save the environment from getting polluted — a very welcome lesson in social consciousness.
- Diwali, thus symbolizes light to glow in our clean life — that is what it symbolizes.

❏❏❏

30. A VISIT TO A HISTORICAL PLACE

It was planned by our school to go out to Agra to see one of the seven wonders of the world —the Taj. The announcement was made in the school assembly by the Principal that students would be taken to Agra and the announcement sent a wave of joy and elation among all of us. How thrilling would be this experience; how exciting how wonderful. We had heard a lot about the Taj, we had even read about it in our books; we had a full chapter on it in our history book, but now was going to be the occasion to really see with our own eyes what we had thus far only heard about or had read about.

It was so planned by our principal and teachers that we would visit the Taj on the 'full moon' night; that makes the great monument look so glorious and so glamorous — it makes a splendid spectacle — that is what our teachers told us. This planning added even more to our excitement. We may be required to keep awake the whole night — but what of that? — one night's sleep to be given up for such a wonderful experience — no great sacrifice.

We were required to assemble on Saturday afternoon by 2 p.m. in the school campus. We were asked to carry our dinner packet with us and the water bottle. We were not to buy any eatables there nor to throw out any thing within the campus of the Taj Gardens. We were also strictly warned not to be veered away into purchasing any items as souvenirs by the unscrupulous and crafty hawkers there who roam around to fleece the unwary. All these warnings and instructions were over and over again repeated to us by our principal and then by our teachers in charge of our batches into which we had been divided.

We had told about this trip to our parents at home and they had given their consent happily for this trip. From Delhi to Agra by bus — it was going to be about a five hours journey each side. We were all assembled in the school campus at the appointed hour, were divided into batches — the teacher in charge of each batch took charge of his batch, asked us to form ourselves in a line, called up our names for a roll call inspected the items that each one of us was carrying and all this having been done, we were directed to board the buses. It was excitement all over as it was going to be a great day for us. Only some of us had seen the Taj earlier but none had seen it on a full moon night. That was going to be a real experience.

As the buses moved out of the school campus, we all in a chorus, hailed the school by its name with 'three cheers' and the journey started. We sang aloud the school prayer. Our teachers joined us and then started the session of songs — some of our companions sang very well — some songs from the popular films and it was all a 'let-loose', atmosphere — we were given quite the freedom to indulge in it.

How these five hours passed we hardly could feel — we were nearing Agra — no we had passed through the roads of Agra and we were told, we were at 'The Taj'. The full moon shone in the sky. The whole campus seemed as if filled with the milky hue. — Splendid was the word which spontaneously came out in one voice from all.

Leaving our buses at a little distance from the main monument we stepped down, our roll call taken and we marched in an orderly manner to our cherished destination, and only after a while we were at the main gate — The Taj, the dream in white marble glowed in the moonlight in its full splendour. We felt wonder struck at the beauty, the majesty and the magnificance of the domed structure. The moon lit campus added glory to glamour — the Taj looked like a white swan stood still in a sprawling lake of milk.

There were fountains bubbling and bursting out all along the pathway. Green lawns flanked their sides.

Crowds of people, men, women and children, all jostling to find a way for themselves — it was a crowd indeed and so many foreigners — so many of them looking at the monument as though completely wonder struck.

We walked, rather rambled to reach the main platform, took off our shoes as was required and placed them in charge of the custodian. We were up on the main platform over which stood the great monument. Four minarets on the four corners stood like sentinels.

Our teacher of history got us to assemble at a place and told us how the emperor Shahjahan, the mughal emperor, had got this monument built as a mausoleum for his beloved queen Mumtaz Mahal and had desired himself also to be buried by her side after his death. So there were the two graves side by side within the mausoleum. We roamed around, were astounded at the beauty and artistry of the fine carvings — how fine must have been those fingers who with so much artistry created this piece of art. Sometimes we saw towards the Taj and the next moment looked up towards the moon in the sky. The Taj looked no less beautiful than the moon in heaven.

It was for us a dream come true — to have come to visit this architectural wonder about which we had heard so much, read so much. Really our country can truly be proud of this piece of art.

On the backside flowed the placid Yamuna, as if with full sense of gratification in the honour of washing the feet of this wonder of wonders.

For full two hours we were going round and round this monument only wondering and rejoicing. It was now getting about 10 in the night when we came down to sprawl over the lawns to open our tiffin packets. There after was to start our return journey.

We did reach our buses casting the last lingering looks at the 'Dream in Marble' that we had seen. We were back to our homes when the rays of the rising sun were looking from the crevices of the windows.

It shall be a memorable experience for me, rather for us all, never to be erased from our memory.

POINTS TO REMEMBER

- Announcement by the Principal in the assembly — a visit to the Taj in Agra.
- Great excitement among students.
- Permission from the parents taken.
- Arrival at the school campus at the appointed hour on the fixed date.
- Students divided into batches, each batch in charge of a teacher who took the roll call of his batch.
- Boarding the buses with their respective lunch packets and after a joyful and hillarious journey of five hours reached the Taj.
- It was full moonlit night — The very first sight of the Taj from the main gate was so enchanting.
- Description of the campus — green lawns and fountains.
- Reaching the main platform after putting off the shoes.
- The History teacher assembled the boys and told them about the whole history of the Taj.
- The beauty of the white marble monument in moonlit night like a swan in the lake of milk. The river Yamuna washing the feet as if at the back.
- After spending two hours enjoying the beauty, had dinner from the packed tiffin box, came back to the buses and by day break were back to Delhi. — A memorable experience.

31. THE INDEPENDENCE DAY

15th August 1947 is a red-letter day in the history of our Country; the day on which India got her independence after a long drawn struggle. The history of this struggle for freedom can be traced back to the first war of independence fought against the rulers — the British— as far back as in 1857. The English historians might have named if as 'Mutiny' but in reality it was a struggle for independence. The causes might have been any but the spirit and the sentiment behind it was to break away from the shackles of the British yoke. The British, with great manipulation and maneouverings had succeeded in establishing their supremacy and authority over India but for that the people of India themselves had been responsible. They stood divided among themselves and wanted to settle personal scores with one another. The British, intelligent and diplomatic as they were, sensed this inherent division and took the fullest advantage of the situation by aggravating dissensions and then presenting themselves as the arbiters, and ultimately the usurpers of power. In the form of the East India Company, they had put their foot on the Indian soil as traders, interested only in the promotion of trade and commerce. That was during the reign of Emperor Jahangir, the Moghul emperor. But gradually this trading company first took the initiative in the financial sector and then extended their scope to political gains and colonial expansion and gradually succeeded in their plans. India at last, came directly, under the British rule and became a part of the British Empire.

But there was a lot of discrimination against the Indian people — natives — as they were contemptuously called by the British. Such subjugation and slavery went on for quite a long spell of time — the unrest in the minds of the people kept brewing up but without any organization and leadership the ambers remained buried under the ashes.

Raja Ram Mohan Roy, Swami Dayanand Saraswati, Swami Vivekananda, The Theosophical Society of India — were the people and the organizations which created a social and cultural renaissance in the country. The Indian National Congress in its initial shape in first three annual sessions praised the British government and only prayed for reforms. It was only in 1907 for the first time that Bal Gangadhar Tilak raised his voice against the British domination and everything Western and it was Tilak who for the first time gave the proud sogan 'Freedom is our birthright and I shall have it'. Lala Lajpat Rai and Bipin Chandra Pal — this trio of Bal, Lal and Pal preached with vehemence to break away from the British shackles. Lala Lajpat Rai exhorted his countrymen in words as 'Indians should no longer be content to be beggars whinning for favours; for, if they cared for their country they would have to strike a blow for themselves. Bipin Chandra Pal — an outstanding Journalist of Bengal wrote in papers like 'New India' and 'Bandematram' which writings worked like a rousing current on the minds of the young people. Certain internal and external factors also worked to arouse the national consciousness and national pride among the people, particularly certain impolite and autocratic steps taken by the Viceroy Lord

Curzon. De Mello — a writer of repute rightly wrote — 'Perhaps no single British administrator in India gave a greater impetus to the national movement than Lord Curzon with his ill-disguised contempt for the Indian National Congress'.

In the meantime there rose up a band of extremist like Chandra Shekhar Azad, Sardar Bhagat Singh, Ashfaqullah and some others who believed in the extreme way of the bomb with which movement the moderates did not agree. The extremists, though failed in their activities, still they helped in arousing the sentiments of the masses. The Jalianawala massacre in 1919 added fuel to the fire. By this time Lal, Bal and Pal had left the scene and Mahatma Gandhi had taken up the leadership. His non-cooperation movement against the British government in 1920, his 'Dandi March' — The Salt Satyagrah and thereafter many more movements carried on the freedom movement still further. The British government failed to satisfy the aspirations for full independence of the country but inspite of making efforts of some settlement, Gandhi turned from the path of cooperation and moderation to complete non-cooperation with the British Government. All efforts having failed Gandhi was led to make the historic announcement of 'Quit India' movement in 1942 and gave the call for 'Do or die'. He strongly pronounced that 'Freedom has not to come tomorrow but today .... I want freedom immediately, this very night before dawn, if it can be had'. This call led to a spontaneous upsurge all over the country — an uncontrolled mass movement at the largest scale. It gave rise to unbriddled violence and sabotaging.

India woke up, as if, from a slumber to mass awakening. The British Government took drastic steps — Gandhi along with all other top leaders were arrested and even the least suspected ones were put to persecution and dire punishment.

The Labour Party had come to power in England and Clement Atlee became the Prime Minister. This new government showed a more favourable attitude towards the Indian aspirations and under the Mountbatten plan India was finally divided into India and Pakistan and the country was granted full freedom on August 15, 1947.

The long fought struggle was brought to a glorious end but at a great cost — the greatest being the bifurcation of the country into two.

August 15, thus is the day of deliverance from the foreign yoke — a great day, a solemn day. This day shall remain the day of great achievement. This day gives the countrymen an eternal call to protect, preserve and strengthen our freedom which has been won after such an effort, so much of sacrifice and such a long struggle.

POINTS TO REMEMBER

- 15th August is a red-letter day in the history of our country.
- The struggle for freedom dates back to the first war of independence fought in 1857.
- The British diplomacy succeeded in understanding the divisions among the people of country and they exploited it to the full.
- The history of how the British spread their tentacles in establishing their empire — first in the form of East India Company and then as a political power.
- India lacked leadership, though there was an inherent desire to throw away the British yoke.

- Raja Ram Mohan Roy, Swami Dayanand Saraswati, Swami Vivekananda created a social revolution.
- Indian National Congress got established and leaders like Lala Lajpat Rai, Bipin Chandra Pal and Bal Gangadhar Tilak took up the scene.The contempt of Lord Curzon towards Indians, helped in fanning the fire of unrest.
- Revolutionaries like Azad, Bhagat Singh and Ashfaqullah took to 'Bomb Culture', but could not succeed except in creating a national fervour.
- Gandhi took up leadership after 1919. The non-cooperation movement of 1920; The Dandi march; The Salt Satyagrah; and then finally the 'Quit India' movement of 1942 — the call of 'Do or Die'.
- The British government under the Labour Party finally agreed to transfer power but it was done to a divided India on 15th August 1947 — India divided into two — India and Pakistan.

❑ ❑ ❑

32. TREES — A BOON TO MANKIND

God has given to mankind nature's treasure in so many forms and in so many shapes but the present man has deformed the forms and mis-shaped the shapes. Mountains and rivers, fields and forests have been assigned by the Creator to play their part for the welfare of the best of his creations — Man. But man has completely mistaken these bounties and misused them in his utter self-interest resulting in the mauling of his being and in the murdering of his self. But the modern man still does not see the doom looming large before him. So blinded is he by the sense of his immediate gain.

Trees are one such boon bestowed on mankind. They form such an important part in our well-being and play such a significant role in our healthy living. But man's lust for more and more of material gains; more and more of land for their agriculture and still more for their factories and industries has resulted in the depletion of this treasure of nature, on such a large scale. The entire eco-system stands disturbed and disbalanced; the mountains have lost their lustre of greenery; the slopes stand staring naked; the clouds float away without pouring down; the fields lie parched and dried. All this because 'Trees' have been trimmed, tortured and truncated.

In our country, our ancients had evolved a method to protect this bounty of nature. Trees used to be worshipped as a deity; there was divinity attached to them; the 'Neem', the 'Peepal', the 'Banyan', the 'Mango', the 'Maulshree' the 'Kadamb', the 'Kachnar', the 'Tulsi', the Amaltash', the 'Ashok' — all these were deified and therefore forbidden to be cut down or even truncated. The Indian pyche, prone to be religious and devout would worship these trees on different occasions and would rather plant more and more of them rather than cause any harm to them.

Lord Krishna, during his childhood played and danced under the shady groves of the mango trees in Brindaban. Lord Rama, during his fourteen years of exile lived in the forests, the grass and shrubs were used in the making of his huts in 'Panchavati'; Lord Shiva has his abode in the Himalayas all covered with forests — that is how the belief goes.

Similarly did the Pagans among Greeks in the Western World worshipped nature in its various forms.

These were the ways adopted by our wise ancients to save nature and to protect the ecological balance.

Man of today calls himself a scientifically developed being and where science advances religion declines. Science relies on reason while religion relies on faith. And here arises the basic conflict. Man of today wants to achieve more and still more — whatever be the cost that he be required to pay for it even if he has to play foul with nature. This is the thinking which has led to the large scale devastation of forests.

Trees provide carbon dioxide as well as oxygen to the environment thus maintaining a balance and an equilibrium. They help in the soil formation and control soil erosion, thus saving the healthy minerals of the soil from being washed away. They impede the flush and flow of the rain water gushing forth from the mountains slopes and thus while protecting the soil, they also save the rivers from getting unduly silted, which silting raises the level of their basins and make them overflow their banks resulting in floods.

Trees provide food and shelter to the fauna and serve as a natural habitat for them. They control landslides in the mountain region helping to save life and property. But very sad is the shape of things in our country at present. Forests are fast disappearing and this is causing very serious ecological consequences adversely affecting India's climate, rainfall and soil fertility. In many parts where the forest area has been depleted, the fertile top soil built up over centuries has been washed away in one season. The regeneration of these lands will become a massive exercise which may well neigh be impossible. The virginal forests offer a strong temptation to encroachers and exploiters. The timber wealth provides a ready and tempting reward and, therefore, is there so much of pilferage of forest wealth and illegal felling of trees. The forest department has neither the means nor the manpower to, combat these 'mafias' operating in this illegal operation. Wood is a precious commodity and the fact of facts is that we are consuming four times as much wood as is being rcgenerated. Afforestation projects are not being able to cope with the extent of deforestation that is taking place. If our forests are to be saved, drastic steps will have to be taken otherwise the malady would reach a proportion which it would become hard to remedy. Can we and should we afford to turn a large part of our country into a vast, and inhospitable wasteland? This we cannot and should not.

Therefore the beginning should be made without any further delay otherwise a stage of no-return will be reached soon. It is not the government alone which can treat the malady and rectify the wrong. A civic consciousness has to be aroused and a sense of commitment to be awakened among the masses to treat trees as a part and parcel of their own family and any injury to them be treated as if an injury to one's near and dear ones Every child in every school should be oriented in this thinking that planting a sapling and nurturing it to its full growth in any part of the vacant land, whether within the school campus or in one's living locality should be treated as a mission of life and an achievement of an aim, as much material and significant as passing an examination to get enter a career. Those harming the flora in any manner should be punished in a deterrent manner just as causing injury to a human being.

One person one tree — if this mission and message can get through — India can once again regain its lost grandeur in Nature's grand show. Plantation of trees is one of the most altruistic of actions. One generation plants them and the second or the third reaps its fruits. So the planting of trees is a divinely altruistic gesture. Let the significance of this great act be understood in this manner.

POINTS TO REMEMBER

- God has given the nature's gifts to mankind but it is man who has misused or deformed them in utter self-interest.
- Trees are one such boon. They form an important part of our well being.
- Man, in his lust for material gain depleted this treasure and has disturbed the entire ecosystem.
- The mountains have been rendered naked and attract no rainfall. Trees attracted the clouds.
- Our ancients had developed a way to preserve the trees. They had given to certain trees a divinity to be worshipped as a deity. We shall not harm one whom we worship.
- Lord Krishna danced under the cluster of trees. Ram lived for fourteen years in the forest in exile, under the shade of trees.
- Pagans among Greeks also were worshippers of nature and had created gods among nature.
- Man has developed science and where science develops, faith dies.
- Trees provide oxygen in the morning and carbon dioxide in the evening — thus they maintain a balance.
- Trees stop soil erosion and landslides.
- Trees provide food to a large number of animals and habitation to birds.

- The land wasted by erosion can take centuries to recover.
- Afforestation is the demand of the day and a civic consciousness needs to be awakened to preserve trees and to plant more.

❑ ❑ ❑

33. CHOICE OF A CAREER

The young men or women of today find themselves on the cross roads when the question of choosing a career faces them squarely. This choice ultimately designs his or her life and can become a boon or a disaster. Very few among the youth of today in our country can say with any amount of certainty or determination what career they are going to choose. This lack of decision on their part makes them a rudderless boat and at whatever shore they reach, that becomes their profession and their career. That is very generally the scenario. Engineering or the medical line was once considered as the be-all and end-all of launching on a successful career. Every parent looked forward to their children getting into either of these lines. But then, for the past decade or more the engineering and medical graduates have been found competing for the All India Administrative Services and successfully too. All those precious years of their learning in a technical branch went waste and the nation's wealth went ill-spent on them and some other one was deprived of the chance who could have entered these professions but missed by a position, which went to those who opted out of it later.

One who failed to qualify at any competitive examination for an administrative service, ultimately joined the law course and later became a lawyer. Among the horde of advocates all over the country, if a census is taken, a sizeable number would be found to have joined the profession as the last resort. Though, of course, many of such proved very successful in this career but that was just a chance — a fortunate chance for them. That was not a career of their choice but they made the best of it and that is what it was.

An MBA degree, a decade or two earlier, was considered to be a surety of a well-placed career but such has been the mad race for this degree and among the institutes opened at very nook and corner awarding this degree, that now an MBA, degree holder except from the top ten prestigious institutes of the country, is going begging for a job and none heeding them.

Therefore, the choice of a career is really a very challenging factor in a youngman's life. Our educational system has hardly changed and there is hardly any vocational orientation explored in the system. The rut, as of old, continues and grinds the young mind in it to bring him or her to a dead end. Jobs are fewer than the seekers and that creates the situation of a quandary. The large scale exodus of the youth from the villages to the towns — the mirage of which draws them — deflects their minds from the land and their youthful energies which could have made their fields yield precious more get wasted and lost in the dark alleys of the towns. Neither do they remain attached to their hearth and home nor are they able to create a liveable home in the town. The type of education that they normally get makes them unfit for the rough and tough of the agricultural life and the living that they are able to eke out in the town hardly suffices for them and their families. The dilemma goes on in this manner.

There have been commissions after commissions which were commissioned to plan out a changed educational pattern for the country to suit its needs and the needs of the youths. The Mudaliar Commission, the Radhakrishnan Commission, the Kothari Commission — all found fault with the existing educational system but then the result has been a return to square one. 'We know the right and do approve it too. Condemn the wrong still the wrong pursue' — this is what has been true of these commissions.

So this has all been the analysis of the malaise. Now let us seek a solution.

The very first reformation that is required to solve the problem is in the system of education. Education is, of course, a must for every young of a nation. Without that there would be no enlightenment and no progress. Basic education has to be a must. But after the junior high school stage there should be a diversification of educational curriculum. Only the scholarly ones should be permitted to go in for a formal education. Technical institutes, as in foreign countries, should be established even for such soiled collared jobs like that of a carpenter, a blacksmith or a mason and only a duly qualified one be permitted to carry on these vocations. Those who be found physically capable of such hard jobs may be allured to join them and a respectable payment to them assured — which alone can be an allurement for them. There has to be a large scale enlargement of such jobs.

For those opting in for the 'white collared jobs', — whether technical or professional or formal, the going should be made tough and costly, and the entry into them made possible only after qualifying at a hard competition. It does not and would not mean that only the children of the rich could opt for such jobs; even the poorer if intellectually bright, could compete for entry into these courses and if found brilliant in competition, they should be granted substantial scholarships for which due provision be made. This would not cause any discrimination so far as merit is concerned. The brilliant would receive the reward for their brilliance and for nothing else.

Professional counsellors should advise in the choice of a career — that system needs to be evolved so that the youth do not go stray in wrong careers. Parents should also play their proper role. They should try to judge the potential and the mental predilection of their child and not force them into careers against their mental leanings. There have been cases where a chartered accountant like Shekhar Kapur becomes a successful film director; a graduate in mass communication like Rinki Khanna enters the film career with success.

The field of information and technology has opened up unlimited vistas in so many diversified fields that more and more youngmen and youngwomen shall find a career in this field very rewarding. More and more emphasis be laid in giving technical training in this field which would not need a very high degree but most of the devices could be learnt through experience. This branch opens up vast vistas of careers — careers not only in metropolitan towns but even in smaller towns even in the rural areas. This is a field which needs to be explored to the full for career seekers.

A carefully chalked out career would make the young mind explore his potential and would make the career rewarding both mentally and financially. That is what a well chosen career needs to do and shall do if rightly chosen. A job-satisfaction to a job seeker makes him to devote his best to the job. That makes the job enjoyable and agreeable and the job, in return, gets the best out of the job doer. This becomes an overall advantage to the nation. The right man at the right place — this if achieved would give shape to a vibrant society. A disgruntled, frustrated, famished youth is a liability to himself and to the nation. Such a situation needs to be guarded against in the interest of the national good.

POINTS TO REMEMBER

- The youth of the country today finds himself on the cross-roads in choosing a career. There is lack of over-all planning. Even medical and Engineering graduates are found opting for the All India Administrative Services, wasting so much of the nation's money on their technical education.
- An MBA degree some years ago was considered a sure passage to a good career but now there is a glutting even in this field.
- Our educational system has hardly adjusted itself to the demands of the age—no vocational courses are generally available to students, ensuring them a career.
- Village life has not improved as much as should and every youth of the village runs to towns in search of a white-collared job. The sort of education which he receives does not leave him fit for the rough and tough life of an agriculturist.

- What is the solution? — The solutions area:
  (a) Higher academic education should be made costly.
  (b) More vocational courses should be started.
  (c) Professional counsellors should advise choice of a career.
  (d) Parents should also judge the potential and inclination of their child and not force a line of their choice on them.
  (e) I.T. technology has opened new horizon and should be further explored.
  (f) The job seeker should find a job which he enjoys — a forced job would be a liability on the individual and ultimately upon the nation.

❏❏❏

34. AMBITION — A KEY TO SUCCESS — A MALADY FOR THE MIND TOO

A man without any ambition is a boat without the sails. It can drift in any direction and at the end of the day may find life a fruitless and frustrated nothingness. There needs to be some point, some direction in life which may lead one on and on. R.L. Stevenson an English essayist has said 'An aspiration is a joy forever. To travel hopefully is better than to arrive'. If one has arrived, the joy of the journey is over. You keep enjoying a journey with the expectancy of reaching. Once you have reached, that bouyancy filling you during the journey is over. This does not, so much mean, that one should not achieve what one wants to but any achievement should not be taken as the land's end. What you achieve today should inspire you to try to achieve still more and still further. That would keep life with a 'living and kicking' sensation and shall vivify you, otherwise there would hardly remain any charm and zest in living. There should ever be a goal to be achieved; if Kanchenjunga has been reached, Mt. Everest still should keep beckoning you. That is what Stevenson meant when he said 'an aspiration is a joy for-ever'. An impetus is the elixir of life and that should never be lost. Achievements have no end, one leads to the next and the next to still next. The joy of winning a race is only when you have a competitor close at heels. A lone runner may grow sluggish in his pace as he will take it for granted that he has won the race. Once having put in his best efforts to win at the national event, you begin looking forward to the World Olympics and even after winning at that you begin aspiring to retain the position even at the next. Why should one try to gain and regain the championship at the Wimbledon tournament year after year and there have been players who have remained at the top for eight successive years. Why give up if you have the stamina but once you give up the stamina gives you up. The Trophies are brought and kept aloft for the contesting final teams to get a look at them. It is to win that they have to fight hard. 'Say not the struggle not availeth' wrote the poet Arthur Hugh Clough.

This is one side of the story. While 'ambition' and having an ambition is something worthy but over-ambition can become 'fatal'. Macbeth is made to say by Shakespeare —

'I've no spur to prick the sides of my intent
But the vaulting ambition
Which overleaps and falls to the other side'

While 'ambition' may be an elixir, 'vaulting ambition' may prove a disaster 'First deserve then desire' — that is what the saying says. Aspire, but while doing so, try to know your capacity and judge your limits. Otherwise 'crying for the moon' can lead to a life-time frustration and life would turn into a tragedy. 'Know thyself' — that is a religious preaching given by saints and sages — this means try to look within you and you will find the Eternal Being within you. That is the philosophical interpretation of the preaching. But in the present context of 'ambition', it may be taken to mean — 'Know your limits and aspire only that much as your limits permit'. Otherwise if you aspire only because aspire you have to, the result can be an everlasting frustration and despondency which would mean 'death' in life. It would become an incurable 'malady' which would torture and torment the mind at all times and in every measure.

Ambitions — the vaulting ones, have led to disasters. History is a record of such events. Alexander the Great, wanted to be known as the conqueror of the world and he conquered lands after lands. But his soldiers and his army had their own limits of sustaining physical strain and at one point of time they virtually revolted and Alexander had to beat a retreat. Ashok had the ambition to conquer Kalinga — hundreds and thousands were butchered. Ultimately, he could find no peace in warfare and peace came only for him in 'Peace'; in 'Bhudham Sharanam Gachchami'.

Such wild and unbridled ambitions have met with such misfortunes and maladies.

So to cut the long story short, it is good to have an ambition which is within ones capacities but beyond that if one goes, malady awaits one — unsustainable and incurable.

POINTS TO REMEMBER

- Ambition is necessary to give a point and a direction to life.
- Eternal effort is what makes life's journey a pleasant experience.
- But 'over-ambition' or 'vaulting ambition' leads to frustration and failure, resulting in mental devastation.
- One must know his limitations and then 'desire'.
- It is good to have an ambition but bad to have a 'vaulting ambition'.

❑ ❑ ❑

35. ADVERTISEMENTS

We turn the pages of a newspaper, turn the pages of a magazine or switch on the T.V. and there are advertisements after advertisements that we come across. We move on the roads and there are big posters and large hoardings that are found put up to advertise products. There are noted filmstars — Amitabh Bachchan, Shah Rukh Khan, Amir Khan, Govinda and so many actresses on the top of the ladder who are found advertising cars, tyres, soft drinks, beauty creams and what not. Iodized salt — Dandinamak or Pan Parag — panmasala, soaps, oils and ointments — all find advertisements appearing on pages of magazines and on the T.V. screens. The producers of these products spend thousands, lacs, even crores on these advertise-ments. The film stars receive more money for appearing in these advertisements than what they might be receiving for their acting roles. Even Sachin Tendulkar — the cricket maestro has advertising assignments for which he is paid heavily.

So what we find is that in the industrial world of today advertisements play a great part. The same thing coming up again and again with its contents and qualities repeated does influence the viewer's or the reader's mind and he feels for a moment — 'why not give a try to it, so much is being said about it; there must be something special about it'. It is this pressure on the mind of the reader or the viewer that is attempted at and it is this psychological influencing and exploitation which is the basis of advertisements. So much is said about a product, about its contents and repeated on and on, and again and again that the mind gets turned to give it a trial.

There was time when as a toothpaste it was only Colgate which was popularly used but now in so many homes 'close-up' or 'Pepsodent' has been adopted. So many detergents are kept on being advertised — 'Nirma' used to be the popular brand used in most homes; now 'Surf', 'Ujala', 'Robin' are being found. So much in use. The VIP vests and Rupa frontline Govinda's 'aram ka mamla hai' has influenced so many minds in favour of what he advertises. 'Apollo' or M.R.F. tyres — people feel like getting convinced of their touchness. The 'Cola' and 'Pepsi' — soft drink war is on and on and both are roping in big names to give their products a boost.

This is an age of propaganda and advertisement. The more one spends on it the more is the return. Public mind is ready to be caught by constant and repeated pressure and it is this — how much one can do it — the more successful is the businessman. Even medicines, pain-balms, tonics — which doctors need to prescribed are advertised as in India a doctor's prescription is not always necessary for obtaining a medicine from the chemists' shop. One is suffering from cough and can himself go and ask for Glycodine Syrup as there is so much advertisement about it; get a pain in any part of the body and go in for 'Moove' pain balm — and it does relieve the pain too. The user feels convinced of its efficacy would tell about to friends and so goes up the popular use.

Houses, flats, colonies — it appears from the advertisements that it is heaven being offered for no price and the prospective purchaser is lured by the details advertised.

And if things and products are not advertised about how is one to get to know about it. Therefore, advertisements are necessary for the seller as well as necessary for the buyer. At least the basic knowledge about the item should be pre-known. This is for what advertisements become necessary.

Big and renowned people are saying 'good' about something; it is not for nothing that they would be saying so. That psychology also works with the prospective purchaser. If Amitabh Bachchan is liking a particular 'Soft drink' there must be something good about it. This is how the general trend of mind works and it is this that the advertisers exploit.

Advertisement has today become a great art and a great science. There are special training and courses in advertisements and it is a specialised field now. 'Catch the mind' — how — that is what a good advertiser should learn and know.

POINTS TO REMEMBER

- Every newspaper, magazine and T.V. carries advertisements — they sustain on them.
- Big people, big money paid to them, — that is the way of advertisement these days.
- The reader's and viewer's mind has to be caught and exploited the most — that is good advertisement. People should be lured to give the product a trial.
- Even medicines which are a specialised field for doctors and physicians also get advertised and people use the products and find them useful. So the trade in them gets a boost.
- If products or items are not advertised about how are people to know about them — so advertisement is necessary for the buyer as much as to the seller.
- Advertisement today has become a very specialised field — it needs training and specialisation — it is an art as well as science.

❒ ❒ ❒

36. MOTHER'S DAY

May 12, every year is a day dedicated to mothers and has begun to be celebrated as the 'Mother's Day'. There is a growing trend of celebrating 'Days' now — the Mother's Day, the Valentine Day the World Food Day and what not. This is what our modern town life in particular has adopted from the west like so many other things — food likings in particular. The Indian culture regards mothers and fathers as Gods — (*Matridevo bhava, Pitradevo bhava*). It is an eternal and everlasting thought and ever present thought — regardfulness to the mother and the father.

The Western way of life is such that as soon as the youngman or youngwoman attains the age of youth, he or she wants to lead an independent life — independent of their parents. And, therefore, they need a day specially assigned when they would particularly remember their 'Mother' — that they have one who also deserves some care and concern. They, therefore, have a day when they would visit their mother, offer her some presents, if nothing else then a bouquet and take her out for dinner and when the 'Day' is done, the 'Mother' is dumped back to her loneliness and seclusion only to wait for a year for the next Mother's Day. The Indian way of life and culture has ever seen so different. Ours has been a composite culture — a joint family system — at least parents are always a part of our life and it is not only an obligation but a duty to look after them even if they live in the village while the son works and lives in the town.

Still with such a culture which rests on the emotional and sentimental considerations, one knows not why our modern town life revels in emulating the West. The concept of a 'Mother's Day' is one such example of the emulation of the West and so is the much publisized, much maligned and much agitated against is the 'Valentine Day'.

Let us at least know what this 'Mother's Day' is all about. the date, of course, is May 12, of the year.

The first celebration of the Mother's Day was held in the spring season in ancient Greece by paying tribute to Rhea, the 'Mother' of Gods.

During the 17th century England honoured mothers by celebrating 'Mothering Sunday' on the fourth Sunday of Lent.

In the United States of America Julia Ward Home suggested the idea in 1872 and perceived 'Mother's Day' as dedicated to Peace.

But it was Auna Jarvia of Philadelphia who brought about the official observance of Mother's Day. She wanted this Day to be a holiday and launched a campaign for it. This she did in memory of her mother who died in 1905 and who had, in the late 19th century tried to establish 'Mother's Friendship Days' as a way to heal the scars of the Civil War in America.

In 1907 Jarvia held a ceremony in Grafton, West Virginia, to honour her mother who had died in 1905. The proceedings touched her so greatly that she began a massive campaign to adopt a formal holiday for honouring mothers and in 1910 West Virginia became the first state to recognise Mother's Day. A year later, nearly every State officially marked the Day and in 1914 President Woodrow Wilson officially proclaimed 'Mother's Day' as a national holiday to be held on the second Sunday of May.

Jarvia had begun the celebration as one to be a sentimental tribute to the mother, but her intent and purpose got defeated when she found the 'holiday' being commercialised. Cards got printed in lavish style and got sold out in large numbers, celebrations began to be arranged on a commercial basis. Trade took away the sentiment behind the whole thought. Jarvia felt so frustrated that she thought that her accomplishment was turning bitter for her. She fought against this commercialisation and even filed a law suit in 1923 to stop the celebration of the Mother's Day. She was even arrested for disturbing the peace at a War Mother's Convention, when women sold white carnations. 'White Carnation' was the symbol designed by her for mothers to raise money to help impoverished mothers who had lost their sons in the Civil War. But she never intended to make it a profit earning proposition and that is what it had exactly become.

Jarvia was never a mother herself. She spent her maternal fortune trying to stop the commercialisation of the holiday and the venture that she had started.

Today countries like Denmark, Finland, Italy, Turkey, Australia and Belgium also celebrate Mother's Day on the same day as U.S.

Why, then should India lag behind — India's big towns have also begun the celebration of this Day on a large scale — whether it is more the sentiment behind it or the profit motive — only the card printers and the celebration organisers would better known.

POINTS TO REMEMBER

- May 12 is celebrated as the Mother's Day.
- India needed not to have adopted it, as our national culture already regards 'mothers' as God but the emulation of what happens in the West has introduced this Day in India too.
- The first celebration of the Mother's Day was in Greece — a tribute to Rhea, the Mother of Gods.
- In the 17th century England honoured mothers — celebrating 'Mothering Sunday'.
- In USA Gulia Ward Home suggested the idea in 1872 as the day dedicated to Peace.
- Auna Jarvia formally called for the observance of the Mother's Day — it was in the memory of her mother who had died

in 1905 and who had tried to establish 'Mother's Friendship Days'.

- Jarvia held a ceremony in 1907 and started a campaign. In 1910 West Virginia formally recognised the Day. In 1914 President Woodrow Wilson nationally recognised the Day.
- Jarvia later found that the Day is being commercialised and she started an agitation to stop it. She even filed a suit and was even arrested.
- Today countries like Denmark, Finland, Italy, Turkey, Australia and Belgium celebrate the Day.
- India had also adopted the Day for sentimental reason or commercial — one does not know.

❑ ❑ ❑

37. WORLD'S FOOD DAY

October 16, is the day to highlight the plight of the Hungry, the undernourished and the malnourished of the World — particularly it highlights the plight of such children and mothers.

Inspite of all scientific growth and so much of food production, so much of surplus food grains, still people are reported to be dying of starvation.

The problem that faces the food front is that of storage and transportation. The surplus food grains in certain parts of the world are in such a quantity that there is no space and no provision of storing them. Then arises the problem of carrying them to such regions where people are needing them. The net result of this confusion is that nearly 300 million of people go to bed hungry. Even those who work hard to produce the food grains remain hungry. 600 million live in the villages out of which 400 million depend upon agriculture.

The U.N.O. has made a survey of the food supply world over and their report says —

"Women do not have the same access to food as men. This Ill-arrangement does not only affect their health but also the future of the health of children ...".

Hunger weakens people not only physically but even physiologically and psychologically and it is a vicious cycle in which they get caught.

Seven out of ten of the world's poor, are women and girls. There is so much of talk of empowering women. If it is seriously thought about, the first thing to do about this empowering would be to serve them proper food and nutrition, reduce poverty and make distribution of food equitably to all — men and women.

What malnutrition to mothers can do is alarming. It can be so harmful for the child that they bear and give birth to. Low birth weight, stunted growth, weakness since birth easy to catch diseases. It even causes the brain to lack development, which makes life hellish.

These are the causes and considerations that have led the U.N.O. to call for a day, to be observed as the World's Food Day and that day is October 16.

POINTS TO REMEMBER

- October 16 has been fixed as to be observed as the World's Food Day.
- What has shaken and awakened the world body is the fact that inspite of all scientific development in the field of agriculture people still die of starvation.
- Storage and transportation are the twin problems.

- Even those who work hard to produce food go hungry — 600 million live in villages, 400 million depend upon agriculture.
- Women do not get the same food as menfolk — the result effects future generation — children — they are born unhealthy, live unhealthy.
- In the field of empowerment of women the first step should be providing them proper nutrition.

❑❑❑

38. NEWSPAPERS — THEIR IMPORTANCE

Every morning a man comes on a bicycle and drops a newspaper at our doors — the one out of so many that we have chosen to subscribe. It is not he who remains in a hurry to reach the newspaper to us, we also in the family eagerly await the newspaper.

A newspaper brings so many different things for so many people and that is their importance. To the youngman or youngwoman in search of a job, it is the 'situation vacant' columns which provide him the needed information, where is what that he or she can try for. There is no other means from which he or she can get so much information. There are even special editions that newspapers bring out giving details of employment information. 'Ascent' of the Times of India is one such special weekly supplement.

To those interested in the news about the political scene, there is all that — all that is going on the political front — national as well as international. How very important were the newspapers bringing news in details about the last war with Pakistan — the Kargil War or the

American attack on Afghanistan in search of Osama bin Laden.

There have recently been assembly elections and the Lok-Sabha bye-elections and how anxiously have people on every street corner could be seen trying to get hold of a newspaper to know the latest result.

Then there are international political news which keeps people interested in what goes on in the world.

There are people who would first reach to the Sports page of the newspaper as their first interest is sports.

The middle pages — that contain the Editorial and the leading article are of interest to the elderly ones of the family who have spare time to go through them — people rushing for their offices only skip over the important news on the first page or those interested in business matters turn over the Business pages but after they have left for their offices or place of work, the elder ones who remain at home take up the newspaper after their breakfast and leisurely go through every page of it — this is a past-time for them as also the full use of the newspaper.

Newspapers are such a cheap and handy means of communication of news and people can easily afford it. What makes them low-priced for the volume of reading material that they supply are the advertisements that they publish. Such large scale advertisements cannot have any better and largely circulated means as the news-papers and are a real help to the business and the trading class. Advertisements of all sorts, of goods of all variety are all condensed in the space of the ten, twelve or fifteen pages of a newspaper and one can know what is available where.

Marriages have been made possible through the matrimonial columns of newspapers. What a great service to the society.

Newspapers have also a great part to play in forming public opinions. There are newspapers which are owned by political parties and it is this medium through which they reach their political opinions and views to such a large section of the reading public. Every political party tries to own a newspaper.

But should newspapers give a political coloured news? That is what they should not. Newspapers are the best means of conveying news and it is expected of them to give news in an unbiased manner. People should be rightly educated — they should receive news in the form in which it is. Even the editorials should be having an impartial view point — what is right should be called right, what is wrong should stand condemned. But this is what does not always happen.

However, whatever it is, newspapers shall ever have their importance; they serve a great social purpose and now with people becoming more and more socially and politically conscious the number of newspaper readers is also multiplying. No other means — not even the T.V. can carry all that what a newspaper carries and conveys.

POINTS TO REMEMBER

- The morning starts with the newspaper.
- A newspaper has its own interest to so many in so many different ways — the youth for employment, the businessmen for business, the politician for politics, the sports lover for sports.
- The details of news which a newspaper carries cannot be carried by any other means and method.
- Newspapers are the cheapest means of information containing such a lot of reading material.
- Great public service is performed by newspapers — their matrimonial columns arrange marriages; advertisements help in conducting business.
- Newspapers have a great part to play in educating public in forming opinions and they should play their part impartially and without any colouring.

❏ ❏ ❏

39. SPORTS IN INDIA

India is a country with a billion plus population but in the field of games and sports it is not able to show up even against countries which are as small as one of the country's states.

At the recently held world cup Hockey at Kuala Lumpur India lost against South Korea and against Malaysia — South Korea, a country of the pocket size. In Cricket, the Indian performance remains so uncertain — it may defeat the best and lose to the worst and then it is argued that cricket is a game of chance. Though, of course, we have the world top class among our players — Sachin Tendulkar to name one in cricket or Vishwanath

Anand in chess, but then names are so few to be counted. The World Olympics come and go and India hardly can take any pride in its performance in any item — getting a bronze here or a silver there is the only achievement for this vast country.

There was a time when India had wizards in the field of Hockey — Dhyan Chand and Roop Singh, the two brothers — but that was so long a time back. Then the world had not caught up with the game and Hockey was treated as India's national game. Gradually countries after countries have picked up the game, developed their own new techniques and are displaying a marvellous achievement.

So what actually is wrong with our sports and games.

During the British rule sports and games in India were just a mere source of entertainment for the rich. The credit for promoting sports and games, then, went to the Maharajas and the Princely States. Maharaja Bhupendra Singh of Patiala adopted cricket, wrestling and athletics. He donated the Ranji Trophy which continues to be played on the national level with pride. The great wrestler — Gama — was maintained and sustained by the Maharaja and became the World Champion of his times — Rustaame Zaman.

Maharaja of Nawanagar — Digvijay Singhji hired British coaches to coach promising cricketers. Maharaja Holkar of Indore patronised players of cricket like C.K. Naidu, Mushtaq Ali and C.S. Naidu. Maharaja of Manavdar, Bhopal patronised Hockey and so did

Maharaja of Gwalior. Maharaja of Cooch Behar encouraged football and instituted the Santosh Trophy for National Championship.

With the dawn of independence and the end of the princely states, though country's first Prime Minister — Jawaharlal Nehru, encouraged sports, still no comprehensive sports policy could be formulated. Private sponsorers continue to patronise games like the Indian Air Lines patronising Hockey, Cricket and Table Tennis while the Telephone industries encourage football. But this does not actually help at the national level. Inspite of the Raj Kumari Amrit Kaur Coaching Scheme or the National Institute of Sports at Patiala, nothing much seems to be happening. The BCCI has huge funds and the Cricket players are getting big money but then it is not one sparrow which makes a summer. And even cricket cannot be said to be at the top of the world.

What our country utterly lacks is a national policy on games and sports. The country's budget comes and goes and no one — no M.P. — no minister, none even among the public raises any voice for any substantial allotment and provision for the promotion of games and sports; while in much smaller countries the upcoming players are properly looked after by the government — they are coached, trained and groomed at state expense. Such a vast country, with such a massive population is not able to groom up even a proper eleven for a team game or an individual or two for individual games. One knows not how Milkha Singh or P.T. Usha or Malleshwari could succeed in their own events at the international level. Their own personal devotion, effort and dedication would have been responsible for their achievement.

What is needed is that the government should give a priority to games and sports as a means of national pride. Catch the player or sportsman young, a search should constantly be on to find talents, and once they are discovered all their responsibilities be shouldered by the government — they should be mentally free from all burdens. Intensive and expert coaching, competition and international exposure be given to these players and athletes — the country should consider them their prized possession and they be physically, financially, mentally be inspired and helped to win for the nation. That sense of national pride alone can inspire them to achieve the best. If South Korea, Malasiya, Sri Lanka, Argentina, Cuba, Japan, Taiwan can come up with Olympic Champions, it is a shame for India not to be able to do it. It is only the will that is lacking not the talent.

POINTS TO REMEMBER

- A billion plus population, India is not able to produce Olympic Champions — it is a shame.
- Once India was at the top of hockey but now even that pride of place has been lost.
- During British rule the Maharajas and Princes patronised games and players and world-class players were produced.
- With independence, no regulated and planned sports policy formulated in the country.
- The nation's annual budget makes no provision for games and sports.
- There are world-class players and sportsmen but they are self-made — no state-policy has groomed them.

- There should be a national plan and policy to encourage and patronise players and sportsmen — catch them young and they be trained, groomed and totally adopted in every way by the state — then only world-class players and sportsmen can be produced.

  Even such small countries like South Korea, Argentina, Cuba, Malasiya, Sri Lanka, Japan can produce world-class players and sportsman — India cannot — which means that the 'Will' is not there with the state.

❑ ❑ ❑

40. FOR AND AGAINST EXAMINATIONS

Examinations have been considered as the only means to judge the achievement of students. They are conducted term-wise, half-yearly and annually. There are percentages of marks fixed in accordance with which divisions are awarded — First, Second, third — 60%, 45% or 48% and 44% or 47% and one failing to secure even 33% is declared as failed.

In the present Scenario of examinations, particularly in the English medium system, upto the 12th. Class students are found to be scoring even 90% or even above and those who secure 70% or less are treated as mediocres. Students suffer a sense of disappointment at securing this percentage and so do the parents. There is a lot of mental pressure on the young mind to secure higher and still higher a percentage. Examination papers have their patterns changing — objective type questions of 1 or 2 marks each for a part of the question paper while some are descriptive to test the writing power of candidates. There are All India Boards while there are State Educational Boards conducting these examinations.

Even for getting into the University or the Colleges offering Degree and Post-graduate degrees or the professional degrees like Engineering, Medical or such other professional courses, there are entrance examinations held. And so are examinations held for services — All India, State level, for Bank services or Life Insurance services and the like.

Examinations, thus are the only way to judge a candidate's ability and mental competence and no other method, thus far, has been able to be mooted out as an alternative to this system.

No doubt, it is very difficult to judge a candidate's competence and his or her mental calibre except by putting him or her to a test — this test can only be in writing — short answers or long answers — that is another question but something must be recorded to be judged.

But is all this good about the system?

It has been found that students or even their teachers select out the probable questions or the type of questions that can be expected in that year's examination — at the lower level — say upto the Intermediate level students mug up the answers, without understanding what they are mugging up and if fortunately they get the same questions, the answers to which they had mugged up, they pour that out and secure good marks. Even, an otherwise, more intelligent students might be found securing a poor percentage. Has the examinations judged the real merit? The answer will be a 'no'; but what is the remedy. What is to be done then to decide the better one? And this system of anticipation of probable questions goes on and on till the highest level and preparations are done accordingly.

All the candidates — they number in lacs — cannot be personally interviewed and questioned to judge their individual grade of intelligence or attainment.

All these compulsions make the examination system to go on in the manner that it goes on.

And then the aptitude, the attitude and the mood of the examiner also plays its part while evaluating an answer sheet. The same examiner, if required to examine the same answersheet again without the knowledge that he had evaluated it earlier may award marks quite different from what he had awarded earlier.

What is the yardstick to judge how the candidate getting 89% marks is indeed lesser intelligent than the one getting 92%?

So all these are the points that can go against the present examination system. With the present system going on there remains so much of pressure and stress over the candidates that even stress — management centres prior to the examinations have come into existence.

What is to be done to redress the situation?

The CBSE is contemplating a grading system instead of a division awarding system. The thinking behind this is the same as in the case of one getting 89% and the other one getting 92%. Grading system may place both of them in the same grade. That may be all right.

But then how will these grades help in the admission to a higher class? There again the entrance test will have to be gone through. The Public Service Examinations hold a Prelim before holding the final. This is more a process of elimination than judging true merit. It is the large number which has led to the introduction of this system.

So it has to be admitted that examination system will go on and cannot be done away with.

The only way upto the University level is to have the Semester system, or class tests on weekly or monthly basis and the result culled at the end of the year. This system would greatly eliminate the tension that candidates suffer from as the examination approaches. But this system would need teachers who should be objective and unbiased and impartial — a rare quality in the modern times — though. But this is the only way to improve the system.

At the public service level standardisation of marking should be brought about. Examiners should be made to sit together, discuss the subject matter of each question and the requirement of an answer for grading — with checks and balances at different levels. This can bring uniformity and standardisation.

Examinations have to go on; the system cannot be given up.

POINTS TO REMEMBER

- Examinations — the only way to judge the achievement of students.
- In the present system percentage of marks puts a great pressure and tension on students.
- Entrance tests are held for admission to Universities and Colleges.

- In the present system probable questions are drawn up and their answers mugged up — examinations do not test the real merit.
- Semester system, monthly or weekly tests should be introduced — this would improve the system and lessen the tension and stress.
- But teachers — the examiners — should be just and honest and impartial.
- The gradation system instead of the percentage system can also be a better system.
- At the Public Service Examinations, examiners should sit together, discuss every question and the requirement of an answer for determining the percentage. Checks and counter checks necessary in the process.
- Examinations will have to go on — the system has no replacement for the present.

❑❑❑

41. VOCATIONAL EDUCATION — THE NEED OF THE DAY

Unemployment is a major problem that faces the youngmen of our country. The reason for this is that there are jobs but the youngmen qualified for those jobs are not available. Jobs are mainly with the private sector and the employers want candidates who suit and fit to their job requirements.

Moreover, it has to be somehow, made to be understood by youngmen and their guardians that jobs are not and should not be considered as the only means of livelihood. The young should be so qualified as to make their own start in life even with a modest beginning instead of remaining unemployed. This feeling can only come in them when they have received a training in a vocation which makes them self-confident and self-reliant.

It is therefore necessary that our policy makers should start more and more vocational training institutes. Dignity of labour should be instilled in the minds of youngmen. Tailoring, carpentry, smithy, motor-mechanism, welding, electrician, T.V. mechanism, — training in such trades can make a youngman self-reliant and self-dependent. With a little capital loaned out to him from Banks, he can set up his own workshop instead of knocking this door and that for petty jobs. A mechanic can earn anytime more than a clerk — only that would need hard physical work.

In foreign countries, higher education has been made very costly while vocational training is available at every corner. That is the reason why after 10 or 10+2 the youngman prefers to go in for a technical training and thereafter sets up his own business. Nothing there is treated as below dignity. This feeling and sense of dignity of labour has also to be taught to the youngman of our country. There are technical hands available even for unlocking locks or moving the grass of the lawn or clearing the blinds of the doors and windows. Of course, there people have a better paying capacity which in our country is also there in a class of society but the willing workers are not there.

Polytechnics were opened but they did not do as much as they were required to do.

What is necessary is a planned manner in which this problem should be tackled. There should be an organisation which may collect job-requirements from private and public sector — collate the data and then arrange for imparting technical training accordingly to qualify the youngman for these jobs. Campus selection may be arranged as is done with engineering colleges of distinction.

In the whole process the greatest problem that would be faced is finding the duly qualified trained teaching staff for each vocation. But once the schemes gets going and catches up and the youngman gets attracted towards it and the parents cooperate — the problem of unemployment would get greatly solved. The needy establishments and organisations will get the qualified hands and the qualified hands would get a job.

It is the government which may seriously take up this plan or even invite the private sector to set up such technical institutes. The fee-structure shall have to be controlled and kept within accessible limits of the lower middleclass — all these efforts if made in right earnest shall be a great solution of the country's problems.

POINTS TO REMEMBER

- Unemployment is the greatest problem for the youngmen of our country.
- Private sector is the major employer but they want duly qualified hands.
- But the youngman must understand that job seeking is not the only means of livelihood. Self-employment should be encouraged.
- More and more vocational training institutes be started — such training taken up by the youngman can make himself reliant and self-confident.

- Dignity of labour — this lesson is the first to be learnt by the youngman no job, no work is below dignity as it is in foreign countries.
- Some organisation which may collect data of the type of job-requirements with private and public sector and training in such required fields be imparted.
- Problem would be of trained technical staff. But once the scheme catches up, it is out of the trainees that teachers would come up.
- This scheme would provide technically qualified men to the needy organisations and jobs to the needy youngmen.
- The government should seriously take up this problem; it may even encourage the private sector to set up such technical institutes but with a controlled fee-structure.

A great problem of the country would get solved.

❑❑❑

42. CARD CRAZE

Let any festival come, let any occasion arrive — birth of a child; birthday of young and old, marriages, or marriage anniversaries, or marriage silver or golden jubilees or days like the Valentine Day or the Mother's Day and there are now cards available for all occasions. There has now started a card craze — must have a card to offer. And the card business is flourishing.

When there was the likelihood of an agitation by some cultural zealots against the 'Valentine Day' which they considered anti-Indian culture one of the prime printers of cards the Archies — went in a special petition before the Supreme Court to issue an injunction against these zealots — the Shiva Sena in particular. The Shiva Sena gave an assurance to the court that no vandalism would be resorted to and the petition was disposed off as not required. The Archies are one such card printers who have made a fortune out of this business — the card-craze.

A card sent even for an apology for something wrong having been done and it was a card with a caption I'm Sorry' and inside it was the citation 'I wish I could turn back time and do things differently I want you to know that I'm sorry for what happened!'

Then there are greeting cards and Birthday cards and marriage cards — marriage cards going into hundreds and with high-ups into thousands. Inviting to attend the marriage of his son, the father of the bridegroom humbles himself to the extent of saying 'Please treat this card as if I'm personally present with folded hands inviting you to the marriage party'.

Lots of literature has gone into drafting the citations in the cards — some examples of a Birthday cards — one from a sister to the brother —

'So, on your birthday

I just want to say that you mean

So much to me —

I'm thankful 'that we're family and I'm especially glad to have a brother like you.

'Have a wonderful Birthday'

'For a Brother who means so much'.

Then it is a Birthday card to a Son-in-law from the father-in-law and the family which goes into great admiration and great hopes — the citation reads —

'Son-in-law you're never too busy, never too hurried to care, you're always so eager to offer your help, always so willing to share, that's why you're remembered for the many nice things you do, and you're wished A Birthday, that turns out to be, a special dream come true'. — Loving Wishes Always.

The Birthday cards from a friend goes into the best wishes —

A one of A kind Birthday —

Filled with Smiles, laughter and fun, warmed with wonderful surprises and many a pleasant movement, and beautiful memories of time spent with near and dear ones …

Then there is a card sent on the marriage anniversary which has all that can be said about marriage and greetings galore —

'Marriage is a precious thing that only Loving couples know —

For it's truly a MIRACLE just how much LOVE can grow'.

'May the love within your hearts blossom and flourish, rooted in the strength of commitment and nurtured by the jobs that can be found in sharing life with one another'.

A girl is born to a couple and comes her first Birthday and there is a ready card for her too from the Archies —

For An Adorable Girl On Her Very First Birthday — How much poetry is there in the blessings inscribed in the Card —

'May life touch your little Girl gently, as she celebrates her Birthday number one and casts her magic spell on each and everyone —

May life touch her warmly as her heart learns to sing with the beauty and joy that discovery may bring...'

Cards for everyone, cards for all occasions — all this needs imagination and innovation — new things said in a new way — that is what a card should be and should contain.

This is how thc business grows; this is how the craze gets bought and sold. Life today has its own spells and the card craze is one such spell that has cast itself on all-young and old. It needs quite an effort on the part of the chooser of the card to choose the card with the right citation carrying the sentiment as desired to be expressed.

POINTS TO REMEMBER

- There are cards available for all occasions and for all persons — young and old —birthdays, marriages, anniversaries, jubilees and then the days — the Valentine Day, the Mother's Day and so on.
- It has grown into a big business and keeps on growing everyday — the modern man has become card crazy.
- Cards carry a lot of literature in their citations and that goes to show the fertile imagination and new thoughts coming up. All cards should have something new to say.
- Cards for everyone and for all — this is how the business grows, the craze gets bought and sold in a big way. It takes quite an effort to select the right card with the right sentiment.

43. THE REPUBLIC DAY

January 26, is the day on which our country celebrates the Republic Day. It was on this date that independent India adopted the constitution in the year 1950. The Draft Constitution was framed and was ready by February 1948 but it was formally adopted on January 26, 1950, declaring India in the preamble of the constitution as a Sovereign Socialist Secular Democratic Republic. January 26 has a sentimental importance for our country. It was on January 26, in 1930 that the Indian National Congress had declared the demand for complete independence in the session held in Lahore. It was, therefore, that India as a Republic came into existence on January 26, 1950. Ever since then January 26, every year is celebrated as the Republic Day. It is a great celebration and a grand show.

On this Day, a special function is arranged on the road named as the Raj path. This is the 'path' which runs between the India Gate and Rashtrapati Bhawan. On both flanks of this broad road track amphitheatrical benches are arranged for the pubic to sit and watch the show which goes on for some hours. Some foreign dignitary — the President of any friendly country is invited to be the Chief Guest, who along with the President of India receives the salute of the army contingents, the police personnel, the NCC cadets, the school children. The whole show presents a grand spectacle and a running commentary over the show goes on which is relayed over the All India Radio and visually displayed on the T.V.

This is the day on which India presents the selected groups of its army-personnel — all the three wings —

the Artillery, the Navy and the Air Force — who march in an elegant manner presenting a salute to the President of India and the Chief Guest who have a special pedestal put up as the central stage of the show. All the V.I.P. and V.V.I.P. guests are seated on both sides of this pedestal. There are contingents of the army cavalry; the Camel brigade which also present a salute in a disciplined formation. Then there are the tabulaes presented by the different government departments high lighting their achievements and the different states present special features of their local culture and ways of life. In this way India as a unity even in diversity is amply demonstrated and presented. The children selected from different educational institutions put up cultural shows on the Rajpath and thus goes on the marvellous and worth-seeing spectacle for nearly three hours.

The most elegant part of the show are the tabulaes presented by the three wings of the army, who put up the latest achievements and acquisitions of the army in the most modern and uptodate weaponry which gives to the world at large a show of our strength as a nation prepared for any contingency and emergency, if ever our national integrity is challanged. This is the only day on which it is done and the public of the country, the viewers on the T.V. screen are given a feel how strong our national defence is.

While on one hand we are shown our strength on the other hand on this day, during the show the highest military awards for outstanding gallantry are also presented. It is a touching sight when the widow of a soldier who gave up his life fighting for the country, comes up to receive the gallantry award on behalf of her late husband. Even children who get selected over the length and breadth of the country for exemplary courage are also rewarded and honoured.

It adds glory and glamour to this grand spectacle when the airforce of the country presents marvellous and miraculous feats of aircraft maneouverings and formations. Even they shower rose petals over the Chief Guests and the spectators which receives a spontaneous cheering.

The whole show comes to a close with the national Anthem — our Jana Gana Mana.

Year after year January 26 is eagerly and keenly awaited for this celebration in the capital of the country — New Delhi and the Rajpath turns really into the Rajpath, particularly on this day.

The Day's show begins with the Prime Minister of the country offering his, and on behalf of the whole nation, a homage to the Amar Jawan Jyoti at the India Gate — this is the first item of the event and everything follows thereafter.

Let us salute our great martyrs first who gave up their lives that the nation may live on. Amar Jawan Jyoti is that symbolic. We are a Republic worthy of celebrating the Republic Day only on their account.

POINTS TO REMEMBER

- January 26, is the Republic Day of our country.
- It was on this date in 1950 that the country adopted the constitution declaring the nation as a Republic. It was on this date in 1930 that the Indian National Congress had demanded complete independence. January 26 has, thus, a sentimental significance.

- The Republic Day is celebrated in the form of a parade on the Rajpath in Delhi — the capital of India.
- Army — all the three wings — Artillery, Navy andAir Force present their show in the form of tabulaes, so do the different states of the country presenting their special features of local culture.

  Unity in diversity is their theme.
- The air force presents spectacular feats with their aircrafts.
- Highest military awards are also presented on this occasion at the parade. Children showing exemplary courage, selected from all over the country, are also awarded awards.
- The day of the parade begins with the Prime Minister offering homage to the martyrs — Amar Jawan Jyoti. They gave up their lives that the nation may live on.
- Let us salute our martyrs who enable us to celebrate the Republic Day with honour and prade.

❑ ❑ ❑

44. A GREAT LEADER

When we are to think of 'a great leader', our mind naturally turns towards a great leader — one of the greatest of the modern world — Mahatma Gandhi. For a political or a national leader who have the turn 'Mahatma' added to it, by itself determines and decides his greatness. No other leader of the modern age has achieved this distinction of being called a 'Mahatma' — one who is 'great' in 'Soul' — 'Mahaan' in 'Atma'.

Let us first know something about his life and how from an ordinary lawyer he grew into a great soul.

Mohandas Karamchand Gandhi was born is 1869 in Porbunder, Kathiawar in Gujarat. At the age of eighteen he passed the University examination and went to England to study law. There, in England, he found himself very much out of place as the society there was quite different from the one in which Gandhi was born. He tried to adapt himself to that society — he studied law, put on the best English dress, even joined classes to learn dancing as the English men and women dance, even broke his vow given to his mother and ate meat. But in none of these ways did he achieve any success and he remained what he was. Only that he passed out the law examination and returned to his country — India — settled in Bombay as a lawyer.

Gandhi had been married, as per the normal social customs, at the early age of 13 years. He wrote in his autobiography how he was deeply attached to his wife. That is what it was but then life as a lawyer in Bombay started well. Gandhi was a very shy sort of a youngman and that was a handicap for him as a lawyer. But then, as luck would have it, he got a chance to go to South Africa as a lawyer to one of his clients. This was a turning point in his life.

In South Africa — under the British rule then, he found that the native 'blacks' were treated by the 'whites' with great disgrace and humiliation. Even he, as an Indian, with a brown complexion, had to suffer this disgrace. He was thrown out of a first class railway compartment by the 'white' Co-travellers as 'blacks' were not allowed to travel by a first class. Having been physically assaulted and thrown out of the compartment, Gandhi at once struck upon an idea which flashed in his mind — passive-resistance — Satyagraha.

From then onwards Gandhi started into a new role — an agitator against racial discrimination on behalf of the Indian Community in South Africa. He made Johannesburg and Praetoria as the centres of his agitation and established a centre for the Indian Community at Phoenix. His tireless zeal in this matter earned him a great name and the Indian Community got a great moral courage under his leadership. He addressed assemblies, was prosecuted and jailed and suffered but would not give up. This strong-willed resistance won him the title of 'Mahatma'.

Gandhi returned to India in January 1915, and soon got out organising the labour class. The gruesome Jalianwala Bagh massacre of unarmed, peaceful assembly at Amritsar turned him to direct political protest against the British government. He became a dominant figure in the Indian National Congress. He launched his non-cooperation movement against the British government in 1920-22, organised protest marches like the Dandi Salt March against the salt-tax.

Gandhi was repeatedly imprisoned for civil disobedience and his final imprisonment came in 1942-44 as a result of his call, to the British to 'Quit India'. So much honour had he won for himself by his selfless struggle that he was invited by the Emperor of Great Britain, King George V to meet him and he met him as he was, in a loincloth and a shawl over the shoulders. It was in this manner that he lastly met Lord Mountbatten and Lady Mountbatten to negotiate on Indian independence.

He had always fought for the rights of the downtrodden and called the untouchables of the Hindu Society as 'Harijans' and stayed with them in their colonies. He always fought for Hindu-Muslim unity.

A man of great moral courage, he fasted so many times, the last being the most dangerous for his life. He was against the creation of Pakistan but then that was done. He still fought for the sake of giving Pakistan its due and this led to a great Hindu backlash. On January 30, 1948 he was killed by a Zealot, Godse for his pro-muslim and pro-Pakistan attitude.

But Gandhi remained an undisputed leader of the masses. His moral courage and his godliness rightly gave him the title of 'Mahatma' and he shall ever be remembered as the greatest leaders of the 20th century.

POINTS TO REMEMBER

- When we think of a great leader, one thinks of Mahatma Gandhi.
- Born at Porbander, Kathiawar, Gujarat in 1869; married at the age of 13 and left for England at the age of 18 to study law.
- Wanted to become an Englishman while in England, tried to learn dancing and even ate meat.
- On his return to India, started practice at Bombay. Had the chance to go to South Africa to plead a case.
- This was the turning point in his life. In South Africa experienced racial discrimination practiced by the 'White' rulers against native 'blacks' Himself became its victim.
- Started agitation against this discrimination and launched 'Satyagraha' — passive resistance.
- Organized the Indian Community in this passive resistance, suffered persecution but did not give up.
- Became a leader with a great soul-force, a Mahatma.

- On arrival back to India organised labourers. The brutal massacre of innocent, unarmed people in Amritsar (Jalianwala Bagh) by the British Soldiers, shifted Gandhi's field of activity to the political scene.
- Non-cooperation movements, passive resistance, Gandhi became the national leader with the Indian National Congress — suffered jail terms several times, undertook fasts.
- Remained committed to fight against untouchability and for Hindu-Muslim unity. Lived a poor-man's life to be an example.
- Did not want partition of the country, favoured Muslims and at last became the victim of a bullet on Jan. 30, 1948.

45. THE ANNUAL FUNCTION OF MY SCHOOL

The year being over, the school arranged the annual function — the annual feature of the school. On this occasion a grand pandal got erected in the school campus with a big dias, with curtains, banners and buntings. On the back curtain behind the dias was a big banner — Annual Function 2002.

The principal had invited an eminent educationist from the capital town to be the Chief Guest. Teachers were made in charge of the different items of the function assisted by a batch of students. It was at 4 p.m. that the function was to be held.

The whole campus and the college building had been cleaned up; the whole pandal was beautifully decorated. Chairs for the guests had been arranged, leaving a passage in between for the Chief Guest to reach the dias. A red carpet was laid over the pathway. Those in charge of the different items of the function had been there since morning, one looking after this, the other looking after that. The teacher incharge of the sound system was again and again testing the mike — with a 'hello', 'hello'. The footlights had been arranged and so were the lighting all over within and without the pandal.

The teachers incharge of the 'At Home' were busy along with their batch of students laying down the tables — the plates cups all in their places.

It was the Prize giving function to be followed by a few cultural items which were adjudged the best in the last evening show. The Prizes were all arranged on one side of the dias on big tables and the teachers in charge were comparing them with the list and arranging them in order.

Guests began to arrive by 3.30 p.m. Those in charge of receiving the guests were busy directing them to the appropriate section meant for them. Students to receive the prizes were seated in the same order in an enclosure arranged for them.

It was time now for the Chief Guest to arrive. The principal and members of the Committee waited at the gate. The Chief Guest kept to time and arrived just at the appointed time. He was received by the principal, was introduced to the members of the Committee and they entered the gates. They were welcomed by the girls dressed in the school uniform showering flowers over them. The teacher on the mike announced the arrival of the Chief Guests; the audience in the pandal stood up at their place till the Chief Guest took his seat on the dias along with the principal and the president of the

Committee. The atmosphere was sombre. Garlands were presented to the Chief Guest by the principal and the president.

The principal took the mike and welcomed the Chief Guest and also the other distinguished guests of the evening. He presented a brief report of the school — its achievements during the year and plans for future.

Then the prize giving function started. The toppers of all the classes were called upon to receive the momentoes. Then a special Gold Medal was presented to the 'Best Student of the Year' for all-round achievements.

The student who had topped at the Board's Examination was worthily awarded a Gold Medal and his parents — father as well as mother were also duly honoured. This was loudly clapped and cheered by the whole audience.

Prizes were also awarded for the cultural show, debate, Quiz competition, on the spot painting competition. It was all so encouraging to the participants.

Then were presented some specially selected cultural items — dances and songs — which had been adjudged as the best. This was in honour of the Chief Guest in particular.

And then the Chief Guest was requested to say a few words. He eloquently praised the school for its achievements and congratulated the boys and girls for receiving prizes as also greatly praised the teachers for their efforts and the principal for his guidance. Then he spoke about education and examinations and made some valuable observations and suggestions.

The president of the Committee then thanked the Chief Guest and all those who had honoured the school with their presence.

The function ended with the National Anthem.

The Chief Guest and those who had specially been invited for it, finally joined at the Tea Party in which students who had received the prizes also joined. It was a great day for them — a great honour; but they had duly deserved it.

It was late evening. The campus stood duly illuminated and all felt greatly relieved — the Annual Function had passed off so successfully.

POINTS TO REMEMBER

- At the end of the session the school arranged its Annual Function.
- A large pandal was erected, duly decorated and a dias with foot lights and sound system — all properly arranged.
- The Chief Guest was an eminent educationist from the capital town.
- All those incharge of the different parts of the programme were busy looking after their part.
- It was the Annual Prize Giving Function with some select cultural items to end the programme.
- Arrival of the Chief Guest, welcome by the principal, presentation of the annual report by the principal, prize-distribution, address by the Chief Guest, thanks giving by the president of the Committee.
- Items of cultural programme presented.
- The function ended with the National Anthem.

  Thereafter the Tea Party with the selected guests and particularly with the prize winners who had richly deserved this honour.

46. TOURISM — INDIA OFFERS A GREAT SCOPE

India, as a country, offers Diversity in its Unity not only in the matter of tribes, communities and religions and ways of life but this diversity also presents itself in its prospects regarding tourism. No country may have so much to offer in the form of historical sites, geographical diversities, climatic differences and nature's gifts as India has to offer.

From the ice-skating and skiing in Gulmarg in Kashmir to the temperate climates of Central India, to the blistering heat of the South — from the palm tree covered Western Ghats and the beaches of Goa to the luscious greenery of Kerala, Meghalaya, Arunachal Pradesh and the beaches of Puri — geography has offered so much to give and enjoy — the variety is so enchanting. Then the religious shrives — Amarnath, Badrinath, Kedarnath, Gangotri, Jamunotri, Vaishno Devi, Haridwar, Rishikesh, Kashi, Mathura, Brindaban, Maha Kaleshwar in Ujjain; Tirupati, Rameshwaram, Kalibari and Kamaksha in Bengal and Assam, Dargah of Salim Chishti at Fatehpur Sikri and of Nizamuddin Aulia in Ajmer, the Golden Temple in Amritsar, Sarnath, Kushinagar, Gaya and Srivasti of Buddhist and newly build Lotus Temple of Bahais in Delhi — these are centres of all religions which call for a visit. The historical monuments — the Taj, Fatehpur Sikri, Sikandra at Agra the Red Fort, The Qutub Minar in Delhi, the Ranthambhor Fort, the Amer Fort, Chittor, and so many other monument with which Rajasthan glorifies itself; go South and there is the

Charminar and the Salarjung Museum in Hyderabad and the Deogiri Fort and the Daultabad Fort, the Frescos of Ajanta and the Temples of Ellora — how many views be counted. They are numerous, rather innumerable.

There are centres for handicrafts from Kashmir to Kanya Kumari and from Gujarat to Orissa and Bengal — choicest products which give a call to be seen and bought.

A tourist coming to India from a foreign land — if he wants to see India in all its aspects must spend a year or two to get just a glimpse of what India's tourist attractions have to offer in all their variety.

India has a vast variety and a great potential for tourist attraction. But, somehow, even when the country has to offer so much, it is regrettable that the tourism department still does not show up that income and that inflow of tourists as it should. For some countries tourism is their main 'export'. The single city of Bangkok attracts more tourists each year than the whole of India.

India has a Department of Tourism, there is the Institute of Tourism and Travel Management, the National Council for Hotel Management and Catering Technology, and the India Tourism Development Corporation. But inspite of all this infrastructure to promote tourism, India gets only 0.4% of the global tourist traffic.

The reasons behind this is lack of interest of foreign tourists in India are — indifferent travel facilities, pollution, ill-keeping of tourist spots, and not a proper planning to guide tourists and give them the proper direction, occasional unrests and terrorism and crime also detertourists.

Such a variety of culture, religion, ancient history, and such diversity in nature's gifts — India should have been the biggest centre of tourist attraction which could have boosted up the nation's economy.

But that is not happening and that is the most unfortunate part.

POINTS TO REMEMBER

- There is so much of diversity that India offers — history, culture, religion, nature, climate, handicrafts — no other country offers so much.
- But the tourism industry is not flourishing as it should.
- The main causes are — indifferent travel facilities, pollution, ill-kept tourist centres, and no proper guidance and direction.
- Instead of any rise in the tourist industry, it is a decline that has been recorded.
- Occasional unrests, terrorism and crime also deter tourists.
- It is really unfortunate that tourism, which could have been converted into a big income-earning industry stands neglected and is on a decline.

❑ ❑ ❑

47. INDIA OF MY DREAMS

May I sit and dream for the best; who can stop me to do that. If not in reality at least in dreams, let me get the best picture of my country. Sometimes, they say, dreams can also come true, so do I also wish.

I have, in my mind, the picture of an ideal India. Ideals may not be real but there is no harm in trying to be real about the ideal.

Politically, India of my dreams would be a successful democractic where all have equal rights and equal opportunities of life. Elections would be held for forming governments but voters would cast their votes for policies and programmes meant for the welfare of the masses and not on caste. If a party with a programme for general welfare comes to power, it would really and genuinely work for the welfare of the people. After getting into power the leaders would only think of the welfare of all people and not on the basis of who voted for them and who did not. It would be the government for all people irrespective of party, caste or religion.

Corruption would be an unheard of thing in India of my dreams. As it is happening today, corruption is like a canker which is eating into the vitals of our political and social life. Not only lacs but crores are being siphoned away from the amount meant for welfare schemes. That is such a black spot on the face of the country. This black spot would stand erased in India of my dreams. Money of the people would be money for the people — taxes would be levied in a judicious manner, no one would try to evade them; pay the taxes as they need to be paid and then the national income thus generated would be totally used for the benefit and welfare of the people.

There would be none naked; none starving, none without a proper roof in India of my dreams. Agriculture would grow, the grannaries would be full and there would be enough for all to eat. There would be a control over population voluntarily imposed by the people over themselves. They would know the value of a planned family.

Education would be available to all and all would avail of this. Education means enlightenment and that is what the people of my India would get. They easily could match the people of any other country in the matter of enlightenment and information.

Industry would develop but not at the cost of general health. There would be no pollution created by the industries — they would use means to control pollution. Cottage industries would be encouraged to give to the rural population incentive to add to their income. Handicrafts would grow and their marketing would also be properly managed. The income would go to the artisan.

India of my dreams shall have a strong military power — as strong as of any other nation; so that none dare challenge my India's integrity and boundaries. Even the common citizen would be possessed with the civic sense and possess a pride for his nation. Socially India of my dreams would be secular but every religion and every faith shall have full freedom to function independently — each one having a regard and tolerance for the other. A social concord and cooperation and a sense of brotherhood among all shall be the hall mark of my India's social set up.

Regard and respect for age, all due consideration for the health of all — the best medical facilities available to keep people free from distress and disease shall be the sole aim of the medical profession. Not for profit but for service — that would be the line on which the medical men would work. The aged would receive due care and as long as they live, life for them would appear worth living. Healthy at birth, hopeful in youth and happy in old age — that would be the way of life of people in the country of my dreams.

Health, Wealth and Wisdom — these would be the key words of life. How pleasant would be the day when dreams as above would be fulfilled and realised.

POINTS TO REMEMBER

- I dream of a country of my dreams, hoping the dreams to come true. Dreams may not be real but what harm if the ideal be thought about and efforts made to realise it.
- Politically, India of my dreams would be a potent, and successful democracy with equal rights for all — welfare of all to be worked for.
- Corruption would not exist. It would stand rooted out. Taxes would be judiciously imposed, honestly paid and the national income would be equitably spent.
- No starvation, no poverty — all to have food, clothing and shelter. Population to be voluntarily controlled.
- Education for all and to all.
- Industry to grow, but should remain pollution free. Cottage industries to be encouraged, promoted and products properly marketted.
- India of my dreams would militarily be powerful — none dare touch its boundaries.
- Socially — equality and tolerance for all religions and faiths and respect for all.
- Health for all — that be aimed at through the medical and health care.

❑❑❑

48. LIFE IN A HOSTEL

Living in a hostel is a lesson in itself. While living at home the young does not turn into a self-dependent being for this thing and for that — for little things even of personal nature, the young look up to the mother or the elder sister. They would keep the clothes in the wardrobe they would prepare the dress for the school and put it in order every morning, they would even arrange the school bag — whether it contains all that is required — the books and notebooks for the day, the pen with ink or lead and the pencil sharpened. The tiffin box should be got ready and then even the study table should be set right and of course, the bed to be put in order. The soap, the shampoo, the powder — toothpaste, the brush — the towel— all to be there in the bathroom. Someone should always be looking after all these items. So much dependence, so much no-care attitude, so much demanding, so much supplying — this is normally to be found in every home. The young grows a little too indulgent.

Sent to the hostel, that one who had remained so much dependent for everything on his or her mother or elder sister or servants, finds himself, initially at a loss. How to adjust, how to manage, how to lookafter every thing by himself. The house-master would come for surprise inspection and he should find everything spic and span, everything in order — no clothes lying on the bed — all properly folded and kept in the wardrobe; the study table properly set — books and notebooks all kept arranged and the pen and pencil kept in the pencil box. The bed should have been well-set — no servant or maid to do it.

So this is a training in self-help which is the first and foremost lesson that one learns from the hostel life.

The other very important training is in discipline. Fixed hours and timings for everything — time to leave the bed in the morning — not that turning over sides while the mother cajoling to make you leave the bed or else would get late for school — none to do that. A quick bath and dressing up, setting the school bag, nothing to be missed.

The bell rings calling each one to the dining hall for breakfast. The same menu for all — no cringing, no crying that you like this and do not like that, or you want this or you want that. The menu, of course, would keep changing every morning — new things added or served but the same for all.

It is a lesson learnt in developing a taste for all kinds of food — a disciplining of the palate, which does not happen in the home. There the mother keeps caring what he or she likes more and what not.

The school hours, the lunch recess, the evening games, the dinner and completing the class work — all has to go on in a regulated daily manner. The mind has to get set to the pattern and any delay or divergence would go wrong.

Regulated way of life is another lesson that hostel life teaches.

The most important lesson that hostel life gives is the training in corporate living — living together. It is a lesson in Social living; in Sociability; in learning the spirit of adjustment and accommodation. This is a great lesson which goes a long way in later life on the Social front.

Hostel life, thus has many things to learn, but there are, sometimes, many things that this life gives an occasion to, which can spoil one's life.

At home, there is the mother, the father, sisters and brothers who give you company as also keep a watch on you. In the hostel if you catch company of bad boys and if there is some laxity in Superintendence you can fall into evil ways, take to drugs or indulge in late night cinerna shows and there is no one so concerned about you as a mother, a sister or a brother can be. The result can be a complete disaster in life.

Discipline is best that comes from within.

Hostel life, thus, has many good things and make one's life disciplined, organised and self-reliant but if the track goes wrong it would mean a derailment and a permanent damage.

POINTS TO REMEMBER

- Hostel life teaches many lessons — self-dependence, self-reliance and disciplined way of life.

  At home the young remains dependent on the mother, the elder sister or the servant, but in the hostel everything has to be done by himself.
- Hostel life gives one the training to develop a taste for whatever food is served. At home one can show his own preferences and throw his own tantrums in the matter of food.
- Regulated way of life is learnt in a hostel life.
- Most important lesson learnt is in corporate living; an adjustment and social accommodation with others.
- There is the other side of the hostel life too.

  Following in bad company and if there is any laxity in supervision one can go wrong, and very wrong sometimes — take to drugs or indulgence into other evils as there is no mother, sister, brother or father to take any personal care about one's welfare.

❑ ❑

49. LESSONS THAT HISTORY TEACHES

An intelligent study of history teaches many lessons. These lessons if properly learnt can make us wiser for life. History has ever been and is a great teacher but only for those who want to learn from it.

History is a record of great minds. Great emperors, great politicians, great thinkers have, through their life and achievements or failures have given great lessons. Queen Elizabeth I of England was ruling in very difficult times when England was badly divided between religious groups. To be a successful ruler, she should have kept both the groups satisfied. So she made a great sacrifice in her personal life and did not marry, as, if she had married a prince belonging to one religion, she would have angered people of the other. Ashok fought a great war but then learnt that killing of men was a sin and turned to become a Buddhist. Earlier Chanakya, the Prime Minister of Chandra Gupta Maurya, guided the king very wisely in the game of politics. Akbar, tried to follow the middle path in matter of religion and became a great ruler, while the Rajputs suffered from mutual rivalry and met with defeat and humiliation. Infighting within always give to the enemy an advantage and Indian history is an example of it ever since the advent of the muslim invaders right upto the advent of the British. Clive could conquer Bengal with just 200 horse men soldiers only because Mir Jafar sided with him against Mir Kasim.

Divided you fall - that is the lesson of History.

Ambitious conquerors succeeded in the beginning but in the end, they all [illegible] their doom. Alexander, the

Great, Napolean, Hitler — they all tried to conquer the whole World and in the early stages became successful but the end of all of them was frustration and even suicide. Their experience should be a warning to all future conquerors and empire builders. Dictators have always met their doom sooner or later and dreams of world dominion have always come to nothing.

Then there is still another great lesson. Wars have never solved problems; rather they have created more. The World War I and the World War II, both ended with nothing so much for the victors. Wars and their results have proved their futility. Neither Russia, nor America gained anything substantially, Britain also lost so many of its dominions — the greatest being India; USSR got dismembered and USA's greatest enemy — Japan — which suffered the greatest disaster is again a friend to USA. Germany which was bifurcated has been united back. So who gained what — none at all. No III World war — that is a clear warning and a clear lesson.

History has also taught us that oppression and exploitation and domination cannot go on for all times. The exploited are bound to react and revolt and sooner or later they will have to be set free. The French Revolution overthrew the autocratic monarch and thus ended the exploitation of the people, the Czar of Russia was overthrown in 1917. Tyranny and despotism cannot go on. Slavery came to an end in USA. India, South Africa and several other colonies under the British rule had to be freed from slavery. History teaches that oppression can only go on for sometime but has to go at last and the triumph of justice and forces of good shall stand.

History also teaches how patriotism stands rewarded. It is one of the noblest of sentiments and stands duly recognised. India is a glowing example. The Indian patriots — how much they suffered at the hands of the imperialists but ultimately they had their day.

Great civilisations have come and gone — the Greek, the Roman, the Egyptian, the Chinese — these were great civilisations in their own times. But now only the remains of these are there as monuments — civilisations have gone. India is the only one that sustains itself but not in the original form, though. All this scenario takes us to a philosophic resignation that nothing — not even the biggest and the highest is ever lasting. Only virtues remain — 'Only actions of the just Smell Sweet and blossom in the dust'.

History, thus is a great teacher only if we are really ready to learn from it. It teaches lessons in morality, goodness, in philosophic resignation as also aggression, oppression, cruelty shall always perish. Sin must stand punished and virtue stands rewarded — life has gone on these lines and let us learn the right way, that it shall go on, and on the same lines.

History — its lessons — can help in the formation of characters, personalities and the people. History is the record of realities but carries us to the realms of idealities.

POINTS TO REMEMBER

- An intelligent study of history teaches many lessons and make us wiser.

- History is a record of great minds, great actions and great achievements but also a record of great failures. Both sides of the picture give lessons worthy of being learnt.
- History has one lesson to give — United we stand, divided we fall — the Indian history is a great example of this right from the muslim invasion to the British rule and even till today India divided into two has no peace.
- Ambitious conquerors, ultimately fall and fail and are vanquished — Alexander, Napolean, Hitler.
- Oppressors never last long — The French Emperor; the Czar of Russia, the British Imperialists — the oppressed would rise up; slavery would stand ended. America, India, South Africa are great examples.
- Patriotism is always rewarded.
- Even great civilisations come and go — nothing lasts forever — Greek, Roman, Egyptian, Chinese — all were great civilisations but nothing remains of them. The world is transient — this is the philosophic lesson.
- Goodness gets its reward, sin suffers — the record of history teaches this.
- Lessons from history can help in the formation of characters, personalities and peoples.

❑ ❑ ❑

50. WHAT IS TERRORISM ?

'Terrorism' is a much talked about term today. And why should it not be when the whole world is coming under its shadow and under its threat. Even the most protected and most technologically advanced country in all modern techniques — America — could be attacked — who then is safe?

But what this terrorism is? The Chamber's Twentieth Century Dictionary definites terrorism as 'an organised system of intimidation especially for political ends'. This, thus explains the mind set of terrorism and terrorists. But today this menace has grown to great dimensions and has taken big proportions.

India has been suffering this menace of terrorism from Pakistan now for more than two decades. Pakistan has, just the one point political agenda, to grab Kashmir in any manner. Having failed in their attempts four times through full scale wars on the issue, they resort to the terrorist activities, sponsoring and infiltrating brainwashed youngmen whom they send on with the lure of big money as well as with a fanatical fervour that they are fighting a 'Jehad', wherein, even if they lose their lives, they go straight to heaven. That is how they even have come as human bombs, ready to blow themselves up in their attempt to blow up something important in India. It was this fanatical move that led the attack on the Red Fort, the J&K Assembly building and on December 13, 2001 on the Indian Parliament. These have been open attempts of terrorism while there have been so many attempts going on in smaller and larger measure in Kashmir. Pakistan has not been able to swallow the political situation of compulsion that Kashmir stands constitutionally accessed to India. India had been fighting its own battle against this terrorism — all the world knew it, watched it but turned its eyes away, particularly the big powers like U.S. and U.K.

It has been when the Twin Trade Centre Towers and the Pentagon of U.S. were attacked by terrorists that the whole world suddenly woke up to the terror of terrorism and the U.S. launched its offensive against the Taliban regime in Afghanistan — targetting Osama Bin Laden as the master-mind behind the attack. The Taliban regime has been finished but Osama Bin Laden has still not been apprehended.

Now the world has come to understand what terrorism is or can be. It is now that the shoe has pinched the biggest world power.

There has been terrorism in India on other fronts too. There was terrorism in Punjab over the demand of Khalistan; there has been terrorism in Nagaland over the demand of a separate Nagaland; there have been and are still the Naxalites operating in the South and in Madhya Pradesh. India has been suffering this diseases for long and on so many fronts.

The LTTE in Sri Lanka is also a terrorist outfit which has been fighting for a separate homeland in Sri Lanka. Their activities have also been going on since long without any cessation or solution. It was the LTTE terrorists who sent the human bomb which killed Rajiv Gandhi.

But there is one point which can be seen as common to all these terrorist activities. The terrorist group got created and got encouraged and ultimately those who encouraged them, they themselves became the victim of those very terrorists.

In Afghanistan, Russia was trying to wield its influence and power. The U.S. could not tolerate it. Afghanistan is an oil-rich country and U.S. could not give that country up to Russia. So with the help and connivance of Pakistan, anti-Russian Taliban forces were sponsored, created and encouraged. And those very forces today made U.S. their target—Russia has withdrawn from there.

Similarly against the Khalistan forces Indira Gandhi created a counter force of Bhindernwala and he, ultimately became so powerful that he became a threat to Indian integrity and Indira Gandhi had to resort to Operation Blue Star to blast the Golden Temple of Amritsar to eliminate Bhindernwala and that ultimately resulted in the assassination of Indira Gandhi by her own Sikh security men.

Rajiv Gandhi boosted up LTTE cadres, had then to send Peace keeping forces to Sri Lanka when the LTTE activities became uncontrollable and the net result was the LTTE terrorists assassinated Rajiv Gandhi through a human bomb.

The Kashmir terrorists also got encouraged when Indira Gandhi dismissed Farooq Abdullah's duly elected government and we are kept on suffering the menace.

So terrorism has been the Alladin's genii who once out of the bottle cannot be put back into the bottle.

One gets reminded of Faustus in Marlowe's tragedy, whom Dr. Faustus creates and that results in his doom.

So this is all what terrorism and terrorists are and have been.

But India has to get determined to fight this 'devil' — it may have to fight by itself — particularly the terrorism in Kashmir. At least the world conscience has also got awakened to this menace and for all that the U.S. and U.K. pronounce, they also at least express their determination to fight terrorism, now that it has struck them straight.

POINTS TO REMEMBER

- The most talked about issue in the world today is 'Terrorism'.
- 'Terrorism is an organised system of intimidation for political ends'.
- India has been long suffering from this menace on so many fronts — North, South, Centre, North-East and has been fighting its own battle against it.
- With the terrorist attack on U.S. the world at large has also awakened to this menace — now that the biggest power of the world has been struck.
- Terrorism, wherever it has grown, the seeds have been sown by those who first encouraged them and then themselves became their targets. Terrorists are, thus, friends of none — that stands proved.
- Terrorism is like Alladin's genii which once brought out of the bottle cannot be kept back in it. It must have its own way — that has been their history here, there, everywhere.
- It is a Political cancer which needs a very deep rooted operation — still will it get cured? — one cannot be sure.

PARAGRAPH WRITING

PARAGRAPH WRITING

Paragraph writing has a still another name and form — Expansion of Idea.

There are certain rules that need to be followed in writing a paragraph. The examiner just gives some subject or quotes a proverbs or a saying and what is required is to expand the idea which is contained in that saying. Something, some good thought has been put in a few words but that may contain a lot of things that can be said on the point.

It is an idea condensed in a few words and that idea has to be elaborated and expanded. While doing so examples can be given, illustrations may be quoted.

But certain things have to be kept in mind while expanding the idea into a paragraph.

The first and foremost rule in writing a paragraph is that the point contained in the subject or the saying should be properly understood. There should be no beating about the bush; the paragraph writer should come to the main central point just at the beginning. No introduction is needed to come to the central idea.

Then, the second thing which has to be kept in view is that every sentence of the paragraph should be an advancement of the idea, not a repetition. Each new sentence should take the idea forward.

There should be a development of the thought — no digression. Unity of thought is the keynote of a paragraph.

Each sentence should appear as a logical development of the idea expressed in the previous sentence. Sentence should succeed sentence in such a way that there appears a sequence which may appear natural.

A good paragraph writing would mean the progression of the idea.

Finally, the paragraph should begin with a striking sentence which carries the key idea behind the subject, the saying or the quotation. That would, at the very outset make it clear to the examiner that the examinee has caught the point.

Thereafter the road becomes clear.

1. GREAT IS ONE WHO GREAT DOES

Deeds judge a man. Actions speak of the character. A man cannot be called 'Great' by his wealth, position of status. Greatness is judged by what and how a man acts in the society, among his fellowmen. A social worker may not be a man of riches but he may command a great respect because he is always ready to render service and help to the needy. Society admires one whose actions are admirable and admirable actions would be those by which the fellowmen stand benefitted; they stand served. Carry a man in pain and distress to the hospital, get him proper medical attention as he has none else to attend on him; serve a meal to one who is starving even if you have to miss your own meal; on a larger scale, set up a nursing home for the poor if you have money and resources; carry on a drive to collect funds to build houses for those whose thatched huts have been reduced to ashes by a fire. Posterity would remember you for these 'great' good deeds. You would have got your name recorded among the 'Great' just by your good deeds — which are 'great' deeds.

❑ ❑ ❑

2. LIVES OF GREAT MEN ALL REMIND US LET'S MAKE OUR LIFE SUBLIME

Lives of great men teach us a great lesson by example. They have done great deeds to be called great and great deeds are always those which are good deeds. Therefore, it means that they were called 'great' because of the good deeds that they had done. Good deed are those which are done in the service of the country, in the service of the society, in the service of one's fellowmen. Such great men become examples to be followed. Man is the best of God's creation and he has the ability to think and to act. Therefore, man should always think good and act good as per the example set before them by the great men. We should make the best use of our lives — that alone would make our lives 'sublime'. This can be done only by actions, examples of which have been set before us by great men. Should we not want that the coming generation also remember us for our good deeds just as we remember the great men? It is, therefore, that lives of great men always keep us reminding us that we also want to be remembered as great men, let us follow the footsteps of those whom we call great.

❑ ❑ ❑

3. HONESTY IS THE BEST POLICY

To be honest in thought, to be honest in deeds — this is what should always be the motto and the guiding principle of our lives. 'Policy' here does not mean any diplomatic action, the simple meaning of 'policy' here is the way of action and behaviour. Honesty always gives a man a great moral courage; he feels a confidence from within that he has not done anything wrong that anybody would point a finger at him. Such a man moves with his head high and is also honoured in the society. A clean conscience is the greatest strength and this comes only by acting and thinking honestly. Never tell a lie, never hide anything, never deceive, never cheat anybody — this is honesty and this is the 'best' thing. Man has been given this life to live; live it so well as on going back from this world you would not leave anything in the form of words and deeds which may give any chance to people to think ill of you. Honesty alone can do it — this is the best way of life.

❑ ❑ ❑

4. SAY NOT, THE STRUGGLE NOT AVAILETH

Life's journey is a difficult journey; it is not a bed of roses. We have to work hard, we have to struggle long to achieve success or to reach our goal. It may happen or appear to be so, that you are keeping on struggling still you are suffering and success still seems far away. People generally lose heart and fall a victim to despondency, despair and disappointment. This is the worst phase of life if one goes through it. Hard work and strong-willed struggle is bound to give good results. Justice may be delayed but it is never denied and hard work always receives its reward. Never give up hope, hope is the elixer of life, have confidence in oneself and struggle on and success is bound to come. Those who get tired shall never complete the journey. Get tired, let it not matter, but do not give up the journey. The destination, the goal awaits the journeyman but it only awaits those who remain the journeyman. Travel hopefully, suffer but do not surrender, let the head be bloody but let it remain unbowed. this is what our leaders who fought for country's freedom have taught us with the example of their struggle. Who could ever imagine that our country would achieve freedom but we have achieved it — it is the great struggle of our freedom fighters who have got it for us. This is a great example of 'Say not the struggle not availeth'.

❑ ❑ ❑

5. GOD HELPS THOSE WHO HELP THEMSELVES

People believe in God; they believe in His mercy — good that they do. But it would be very wrong to think that it is God who has given us birth in this world and it is He who should look after us. Such a thinking and philosophy is self-defeating and thoroughly ill-thought. God has given us birth and has equipped us with a body, a mind and a soul. These are like gifts given to us by God. If one has got wealth and one locks it up in the bank locker without putting it to any use or does not want to use it, what would be the result. Such a one shall have all in his shelf but would die of starvation. Who can help such a fool? Similarly, God would also only help the doer and not the dullard, not the idler. Make your own efforts, struggle hard and then only shall you be rewarded. And that of course is, unless God wants you to be rewarded, you cannot be rewarded. Call it destiny if you choose to but that is what it is. You sow the seed but before it, you have to work hard to till the soil, to plough the fields. And even after sowing the seed you have to give the sprouts due care, water them at intervals, clean the weeds, save the plants from birds and animals — all this hard labour alone can provide the crop and fill in your granary. If you think that you have sowed the seed, your job is over now God should help to do the rest, that is not going to happen. Even the food served before you would reach your month only when your hands, your fingers carry them up. God would not come to feed you. So depend upon your own efforts and pray to God to let you succeed. Many things are wrought by prayer too, but not just by prayer. Your efforts are primary, prayers then are the secondary support. God helps but helps only those who help themselves.

❑ ❑ ❑

6. CHARACTER MAKES A MAN

Character of a man is the combination and collection of many qualities and traits — nature, personal appearance, way of behaviour and mental reactions to situations and circumstances. As soon as we talk of character, immediately the consideration of moral and immoral comes into play, so does strong and weak. What is moral and immoral concerns the society in which one lives and moves but then what is essentially immoral cannot become moral in any society. So whatever character one possesses would be reflecting the man. It is on the basis of the character that a man would be judged. Character is the index of a person's state of mind. There can be situations which some people might badly face while there be some who may begin shaking in their shoes. Judging from this reaction it would be said that the one has a strong character while the other has a weak character. There can be a person who might easily get influenced by the opinion of other people while there would be one who would hold on to his own opinion. The one will be called as a man of weak will while the other of a strong will. Will power is a very important factor in determining character. In this way it is on the basis of one's character that a man would be judged — character reflects the man and man is reflected in the character.

7. SWEET ARE THE USES OF ADVERSITY

'Every cloud has a silver lining' — that is how a saying goes. Adversity — Suffering and Poverty — has also its advantages. Suffering brings out in man's character his capacity to endure; his strength of character and his self-confidence. When a man is doing well, he feels that the world is all good and pleasant. He hardly knows what suffering is or can be. Everything seems so rosy and cosy in life. But when one falls into adversity, one has to gird up his loins and face the realities, stand up to them and to fight them through. There are some who would just surrender to sorrows and lose all courage and whine and weep — they are the chicken hearted persons who crumble and crash with the little pressure. They hardly deserve to be a man. Those who stand up to face the misfortune are men of faith and fortitude — they have faith in themselves and faith in God — they know that even the worst turns into the best. Life is a story of ups and downs — that is how they take the moments or the period of adversity. Adversity also puts to test so many things. It puts to test your friends too. Prosperity wins friends, adversity tests them. True friends are those who would keep up their closeness even during the period of adversity of their friend. Thus, adversity has its own 'Sweet uses' — it puts to test a man's own character; his courage and his confidence in himself as also it puts to test the world around. Life's path has ruggedness too and that also has its lessons to give; if one walks on that path for sometime and thereafter reaches the golden goal, how pleasant does that seem. One judges the goodness by contrast. If the clouds are not dark the flash of lightening would not be dazzling. Misfortunes make the return of fortunes look so pleasant — these are sweet uses of adversity.

❑ ❑ ❑

8. A STITCH IN TIME SAVES NINE

Action at the right and required moment saves a lot of bother in future. Delayed action, adds to the problems and aggravate them, whereafter it becomes so difficult to deal with them or tackle them. This saying has a very rational meaning. Your shirt gets a little torn at a place as you scratched against a thorny bush. Just on reaching home you take it to the darner — it may even be your mother and sister — and she just nicely puts a few stitches and it all looks in order. If that is not done in time the torn part may further increase and then it may become difficult to repair it and give it the decent wearable look. One catches cold and develops a sore throat. You at once soothe it with a hot water saline gargle and by morning you would find yourself relieved. Or you just take on antibiotic tablet and you are well for your morning work. But you grow lethargic, postpone the gargle or the taking of the tablet, you keep coughing throughout the night and find yourself running slight temperature in the morning. Urgent matters, required to be attended to in the morning and the day have to be put off — may be you have lost a job for the interview of which you were to appear at ten in the morning. Just a little care would have made you feel well as also might have got you the job — you have failed on two fronts just by failing in little timely action. And now it has taken you three days to recover from cough, cold and fever. A stitch in time would have saved you from nine. Timely action may need a little effort but saves a lot more efforts which may be forced upon by this in-time neglect.

❑ ❑ ❑

9. COWARDS DIE SEVERAL TIMES BEFORE DEATH

In this world everything is uncertain but what is certain is Death. One who has been born would and must one day die — sooner or later. It is not only man who is mortal but everything is transitory — short-lived. But even knowing full well that death is certain a man with a brave heart faces all the calamities and misfortune boldly. He faces risks, he faces dangers, wins over them and achieves success and as long as he lives, he lives with courage and confidence. That gives a strength to life and to living. But those who are cowards, surrender at every turn of events, get sorrow-stricken and lose all hope. They are virtually dead though living. In this way they have died so many times in life; for what is death? — inaction and inability to have nerves awake and alive. Their spirits are damped, they have lost all hopes. Hope is the elixer of life. That always enlivens one's spirits even in the face of dangers and discouragement. The brave man does not sit brooding over the past, has faith in the present and hopes for the best in future. But coward falls flat at the very first blow and has no will to live, no zest for life — this is virtually death, what else. Such occasions come in the life of a coward many a times in life — so he has died a thousand times though still breathing only. Life has been given to be lived and to be lived well. Do not think of death, do not wait for it — let it come when it may — so long the blood runs in the veins, so long breath is being puffed in and out, look up and face — pleasures and pain alike.

❑ ❑ ❑

10. STRIKE WHEN THE IRON IS HOT

Everyone wants success in life and this can only be when one takes full advantage of the chance that comes in life. Never miss a chance; a little chance can turn into a golden gift. Make the best use of opportunities as opportunities do not always come. The saying as it stands, relates to the work of an ironsmith. The ironsmith sits by the side of his furnace heating the iron rod till it becomes red-hot. That is the right time when he should strike it and mould it in whatever shape he wants. If he misses that chance and allows the red-heat to cool down, the iron would again turn hard and will not be malleable. He will again have to undertake the same process and the same labour —doubling the effort only due to the missed chance. This is an example which has a lesson to give. Make the best of the present; use all your effort, efficiency and skill to turn the opportunity which has come your way, to your advantage. Lethargy, languidity and lengthening of time may prove counter productive. The wise always remain alert and alive — the right thinking man always strikes when the iron is hot. Shakespeare has said the same thing in his play Julius Ceasar when he wrote —

'There is a tide in the affairs of men
Which, taken at the flood, leads on to fortune;
Omitted, all the voyage of their lives
Is bound in shallows and in miseries.

❑ ❑ ❑

11. LOOK BEFORE YOU LEAP

What is being advised through this direction is that man should always carefully plan all his future actions. Deciding to do anything one should always view all sides of the matter, consider all the pros and cons of the consequences before taking that decision. Actions should not be taken in a haste; major or even minor decisions should be considered and judged from all angles. Just as when we walk on the road we take care of the pits or puddles. We do not drive our car blindly or rashly without caring what blockades are there on the road; which part of the road is without pits — this is done for the safety of the car as well as for those who are travelling by it. So it is, while taking a jump, as and when one be required to, one must take due care that one does not fall into a shrub, a thorny bush or a deep crevice. Move with eyes open — that is what is being advised. You are going in to purchase a house. You must take due care of the locality; the surroundings, the environment around; you may even make due enquiries about the neighbours — their nature and their ways. It is the house in which you have to live — it is the quality of material used in its construction, the size of rooms and other amenities that you may look into — why the surroundings or the neighbours. But we do it and that is right doing so. Bad neighbours can make life miserable, unhealthy surroundings can ever be a health hazard. This is going to be a life's purchase — a house is not bought every day — you have to take all this care. This is what 'looking before leaping' would mean. Even in one's talks one must take care of the words that one uses. An unseeming remark or an unbecoming expression can lead to a great crisis in personal relations. So words, acts, decisions — all need to be weighted well before spoken or done or taken.

❑ ❑ ❑

12. LIVE AND LET LIVE

Social life depends upon this concept of 'live and let live'. Society means a group of people living together. Every person has his own likes and dislikes, his own tastes, his own temperament. Therefore, it is necessary that to have peace in life, co-operation and concord, each one should take due care of the other so that life may go on happily and nicely. For doing so one must have a spirit of adjustment and accommodation. One should not try to impose one's own will over other. This is equally true in the world community. One nation should let the other nation have its own freedom. Democracies have to live with dictatorships; Socialism has to live with imperialism. This is what is meant by peaceful co-existence. Violence and dominance is never permitted — neither in individual life, nor in social life, nor in national life, nor at all in international life. Live your own way and let others live their own — that alone is the principle of good living. 'Do not do unto others what you do not want to be done to you' — this is what Christ said. That is the principle of life which alone can make life peaceful and peace brings happiness. Do we not want to live happily? If we want to, others also want the same. That is possible only when you 'live and let live'.

❑ ❑ ❑

13. WORDS HURT MORE DEEPLY THAN WEAPONS

Man is the only speaking animal. Speech is given by God only to man. But it is for man to use that speech in the right proper manner. A wrong word; an abusive expression can cause havoc — it can lead to a quarrel; it can lead even to violence and assault. A courteous expression can win you friendship and goodwill while a discourteous one can cause all the complications and bickerings. A bad word would hurt the mind, a weapon only hurts the body. A wound caused by a weapon may be treated and can heal up and get cured but an injury to the mind and heart goes so deep that it may never be cured. When Duryodhan in Mahabharata mistook the flooring of the beautiful palace as if there was the simmering water or he fell into water considering it as a mirage, Draupadi laughed and mocked at him with the words that 'a blindman's son is blind' — the words got deeply stuck in Duryodhan's mind and that lead to the great war — the Mahabharata. The attempt at disrobing Draupadi after losing the game of dice by Yudhishthira was just a revenge on the part of Duryodhan for Draupadi's words of mockery which had hurt him deep. So the wounds of words go that deep. Politicians, in particular, have to be very careful with words. Their words can make or break empires. Porus got defeated at the hands of Alexander and when brought as a prisoner, Alexander asked him, 'What sort of behaviour should he met with'. And Porus gave a very honourable reply 'As a king should treat a king' — and Alexander was deeply impressed and Porus was let off. A word of respect to elders, a word of courtesy to the neighbour can earn great good will while a disrespectful word or a discourteous address can cause everlasting discord. Words — sharp — can hurt deep; words — soothing can heal wounds.

❑ ❑ ❑

14. ALL THE WORLD'S A STAGE

We are born in this world and are designed and destined to play our part. Whatever part has been allotted to us, that has to be played well and it is only then that it would be said of us that we lived well. People would remember us and we would leave our footprints on the sand of time. A father, a son, a brother, a sister, a neighbour, a leader, a teacher, an industrialist, a business-man, a political leader — all these are parts that destiny has designed for man in the same way as the director of a drama assigns very actor a role for which he be found suitable. The role thus assigned, if properly played leaves a lasting impression on the audience and he is ever remembered for his part. The show goes on, one actor comes, plays his part and goes out and then the other actor comes. Each one keeps playing his part and leaves the stage for others to come and play their part. This is how the world has gone on for thousand, millions and billions of years and shall go on till eternity — one knows not for how long. The poet writes about a rivulet — makes the rivulet to say — 'Men may come and men may go But I go on forever.' So does the world say, about its stage. Generations will come generations will go — no one is immortal — but the world would go on. The stage of the world's theatre shall never be empty of actors. But each one will be playing his own part assigned to him for as long as his part is required in life's drama. This is how we say — 'All the world's a stage'.

❑ ❑ ❑

15. LIBERTY IS NOT A PERSONAL AFFAIR; IT IS A SOCIAL CONTRACT

In a contract, there are always two parties and the contract gets signed only when both the parties agree to its provisions. Similarly life in the society is also a contract between the individuals who form the society. Each one has to take due care that the other one agrees to your way of life, your way of thought, your way of behaviour — one to the other. While doing so it happens that one's thoughts, actions and behaviour have to be adjusted with the thoughts, actions and behaviour of others — it is only then that social life can go on smoothly; the contract can stand in order. But in doing so one must make adjustments, one must accommodate others. It is like this. While travelling in a bus or a train if there is a seat for two, the third man can be offered a corner of the seat but only if the two ones already sitting squeeze in a little — make a little adjustment, curtail their liberty of comfortable sitting. So does it happen in the society. You have the liberty to dress yourself in whatever manner you please — you can just be in a vest and shorts while within your home but coming out on the road you have to take care that you are fairly decently dressed. You can play upon your violin in your home but you cannot go up on the top roof at midnight with your orchestra and play at full volume. The neighbours have a right to a sound undisturbed sleep even though you have the liberty to play upon your instrument. They have the liberty and right to sleep. It amounts to this that your liberty gets curtailed to accommodate the liberty of others. The road is there for everyone to move, but the rule of the road demands you to move on your left and not anywhere and everywhere, otherwise there would be confusion, collision and chaos. Liberty is, therefore, everybody's — it is personal liberty, but it has to be accommodative of other people's liberty. That alone would allow social life to run smooth.

❑❑❑

16. PATRIOTISM IS NOT ENOUGH

Love of one's own country is called 'Patriotism'. Every one has the right to love his country, rather everyone should have a love for his country. W.H. Long fellow — the poet has gone that for to say —

'Breathes there the man with Soul so dead
Who hath not to himself hath said
This is my own, my native land

A man, according to the poet, is 'dead' of 'soul' if he has not within himself the love of his land. It is patriotism which has inspired martyrs to give up their lives for the sake of their countries; in the service of their countries; in fighting for the cause and liberty of their country. Their names stand recorded in golden words in the history of their nation. But then there has to be an adjustment struck with the patriotism of other nations and their nationals. The patriotism of one should not become so aggressive as to deprive others of their freedom. Others have the equal right to love their own country and one country, in its undue zest for his love for his own country cannot encroach upon the freedom of other countries. Napolean did that, Hitler did that — they loved their country, it was all right. For Hitler, Germany was the fatherland but what right had he to try to tread upon the liberty of other nations which he did. Patriotism for him was all right but he had to honour the patriotism of the nationals of other nations too. Similarly Pakistan is launching an offensive against India through infiltrators encouraged and sponsored by it and miscall them 'freedom fighters'. Therefore, Patriotism is a noble sentiment but on the international scene it is 'not enough'; it has not to go to the extent of encroaching upon the liberty of other nations who have an equal right to Patriotism. Aggression in the garb of Patriotism cannot be tolerated, cannot be permitted. Love your own country but keep that love within limits of your own country, serve it well, do everything for its upliftment and its people but do not step over to try to extend your boundaries in the name of Patriotism. Internationalism shall never permit such a patriotism.

❑ ❑ ❑

17. 'A LILY OF A DAY IS FAIRER FAR IN MAY'

Life if given not only to live for ones ownself; it is given to spread love and light to others too. One who does that lives long even after he is gone. Even a short life, just like that of a Lily flower, which just lives for a Day, is so meaningful. The lily of the garden which blossoms with the first rays of the sun in the morning and fades and falls by the evening pleases so many hearts; so many eyes. It is a life well lived though so short — just a day long. Living long but lending no zest, no joy to any one is living a useless life — a life of no achievement, a life of no pleasure, a life of no service. So what such a life is — lost and forgotten in the hazy past with no memories left worth remembering. So life's every moment should be lived for others, to give something, to lend something, to leave something to be remembered by. Even a short existence but with such an achievement is worthier than a long, insipid life lost 'unheard, unhonoured, and unsung'.

❑ ❑ ❑

18. WHAT IS THIS LIFE SO FULL OF CARE WE HAVE NO TIME TO STAND AND STARE

(W.H. Davies)

Wordsworth, the great English poet had earlier said in one of his Sounets, 'The world's two much with us,

Getting and spending we lay waste our powers.
Little do we see in nature that is ours ...'

It is the same idea which the poet W.H. Davies has expressed in the above noted couplet. God has created the whole world of Nature for us; there is so much of charm, so much of beauty; so much to enjoy and at the same time so much to sit and contemplate over these beauties and these bounties of nature. The charming dawn at the crimson horizon every morning; the sun sinking gradually in the sea at a sea-beach; the floating clouds with queer formations; the glorious full moon showering its coolness and its milky moonlight, the twinkling stars; the rising snowcovered mountains — with how much and with what varieties has nature opened its basket of gifts. But the man of today, always in a haste, always in a hurry to rush on to office or to his workplace, keen to earn more and still more, has hardly any time to enjoy these boundless beauties of nature which lie bare before him. Life in the world is ruffled; it is all full of care and concern — to do this, to do that and the poet laments 'we have no time to stand and stare'. And rightly does he lament that. Coming closer to nature, watching its beauty gives a soothing balm to the otherwise battered being of a man. Not only that 'to stand and stare' at the store of beauties laid bare before us leads the mind to the realms of the infinite — who has created all this? Wherefrom has so much of beauty come? Who is the creator? — not of course man — then who? The mind sores high into the higher realms of thought and man's soul feels enlightened and invigorated in solving the mysteries of the universe. Otherwise what happens is that man keeps running after the temporal attractions which are found to be elusive and temporary — what today is, will not be tomorrow, still we hanker and hunt after it. While the sun, the moon, the sky, the stars have ever been there and shall ever be there they are eternal and everlasting. We, of this world, run after the shadow and lose sight of the substance and life which is short ends in this mad pursuit. Nothing is gained, nothing is got. Life full of care — care for money, care for the family, care for the fellows — Care, Care and Care — the net result is that care leaves us bruised and battered and we, by our own fault, lose the touch of the soothing balm which God has given to us as a boon in the form of so much beauty, so much mystery. There is all the philosophy, there is all the religion — it ultimately leads to only one thing — God — who? What? where? Nature offers the answer — He is here, there and everywhere. But this needs a mind and a spirit to watch and see and feel. World and its cares take all our time and attention. Empty handed we came, empty handed we go — nothing gained, nothing got. All time lost.

❑ ❑ ❑

19. STONE WALLS DO NOT MAKE A PRISON NOR IRON-BARS A CAGE

Man has been given a body, but he has also been given a mind and a soul. It is only the body which can be put in a prison or behind iron bars. But none can stop the mind to travel and the soul to soar high. Jawaharlal Nehru was imprisoned by the British for his struggle for country's freedom struggle but it was from behind the prison walls that he wrote down 'letters to his daughter' which became 'history'. Who could stop him to do this writing? The mind was a free bird. Lokmanya Tilak was imprisoned in the Mandalay Jail in, then — Burma and while there, he wrote down his treatise on Bhagwat Gita which is a monumental work. There have been many more such examples of great writers, great thinkers who penned down their thoughts from behind the 'stone-walls'. Mahatma Gandhi did that from the Yarwada Jail. So it is that none can bind down the mind and thoughts. The soul of a man is ever free — stone walls or an iron-cage do not hamper its flights and its force. But there can be persons who may be physically free but mentally they are slaves. They cannot think for themselves; always depend upon other's opinions or are always slaves to other people's commands. It is actually the mind which is the seat of freedom and not the body. To a man whose mind is chainless, a prison is just a hermitage.

❑ ❑ ❑

20. THOSE WHO LIVE IN GLASS HOUSES SHOULD NOT THROW STONES ON OTHERS

All men are liable to commit mistakes and fall a victim to follies. this makes man's position weak and vulnerable. Therefore, one must be very cautious and careful in casting aspersions on others or finding fault with others. The other man so criticised can also find faults with you. So if you are living in a glass house, which means if you have faults with you, your position is as weak as one living in a glass house and if stones are thrown at you your glass house would also get broken and you would stand exposed. Therefore, one needs to be very careful before casting blames on others, or finding faults with them if you yourself suffer from faults and frailties. It is not fair for the pot to call the kettle black as both have been on the fire and both have the black spots over them. Those who are themselves corrupt should take care not to call others corrupt otherwise the other would bounce back. It is only when one is fully convinced of his own honesty and truthfulness that one should dare to accuse others — otherwise it is best to keep quiet.

❑ ❑ ❑

21. SPEECH IS THE GIFT OF ALL BUT THOUGHT OF FEW

Man has been gifted by God with the gift of speech — except one who may be born dumb. Tongue is a supple organ and is ever ready to move; sometimes it moves too fast. People talk and sometimes begin talking a lot and one who talks a lot does sometimes talk irrelevantly and even irresponsibly. Words come out and speech comes out naturally to man. So everyone has the power to speak but few have the soundness to speak thoughtfully. Man is also gifted with the quality of reason. He is the only rational being. So he should make full use of his rational quality before giving his thoughts a speech. Thoughtless speech can create great complications. Even just a slip of the tongue on the part of a politician can create national or even international turmoil. Every word should be measured with thought before being expressed. People, unthinkingly first speak out, and then have to come with a thousand explanations that they did not mean this, they did not mean that. This, so often, keeps happening with political statements — once the statement is carelessly made then explanations are offered that the statement has been misquoted or has been taken out of the context. Recklessness in speech can have disastrous results. Therefore, 'reason' — the gift given to man by God should always be made full use of in speaking out. Cool and considered thinking before giving expression to one's thoughts is the quality of the wise. Speech should be used sparingly only when required like the money kept closed in the iron-safe of a miser.

❑ ❑ ❑

22. A SLAVE IS ONE WHO CANNOT SPEAK HIS THOUGHTS

Slavery does not only mean slavery of the body. As and when slavery existed in the society the slave had no existence of his own — neither physical nor mental. He could neither move nor speak without the sanction of the master. Now, of course, with the change of times, slavery of the body has largely been eliminated from the society. Still there are people, who dare not talk freely; there are wives who would look up to their husbands for anything to say, speak or suggest. There are children who remain scared of their parents and cannot speak out their mind. Though, it is always good to speak in one voice on certain issues in the family or among friends but not so always as to feel scared of voicing one's failings. Such a scare amounts to a worse slavery than even the physical one. Thoughts brew up in the mind; opinions on matters arise in thoughts but for the fear of some one, one cannot express them — may it be the fear of the husband for the wife or the fear of parents for the children or the fear of the boss for the assistant — but mental slavery is what stuns the mind and does not allow it to grow. An expression of opinion, of course, with all due regard towards the one spoken to; a free — expression of thoughts is a great exposure of personality, which is necessary for a rational mind — even if it be of a child. There should not be a constant scare — that is the worst — the worst phase of mental slavery and should always be discouraged. Let the free breeze of thoughts flow from all directions that alone can keep the mental horizon free from haze.

❑ ❑ ❑

23. MAN DOES NOT LIVE BY BREAD ALONE

Man is essentially an animal and has all those physical needs which an animal has eating, drinking and sleeping. But if that be the be-all and end-all of human life; human life would hardly be a worthy gift of God to man. Man is a rational animal; he is a thinking being a feeling being. He is endowed with a mind and a soul. He has the mental strata as well as a moral strata. He should think, plan and achieve. He should aim at progress, at upliftment and at advancement both at the mental level as well as at the moral level. If that is not done and mere eating and drinking — just the bread — is his aim and final objective in life then he has wasted himself. Society needs sentiments, sentiments need emotions, emotions need interaction and relationship — that makes up the total scene of human life. If man would not have thought and planned, no discoveries, no inventions, no growth would have been possible. There would have been no literature, no philosophy, no religion, no morality, no spirituality. Man needs all these they are the means of his sustenance — they are the meaning of his existence. So it is that man, if he is a man and wants to be a man—shall not live by bread alone — though bread may be the basic need but that is not all and everything for human life.

❑ ❑ ❑

24. MAN IS THE ARCHITECT OF HIS FATE

There are men who just resign to whatever comes — they say 'it was so destined, it was so fated'. This is the defeatist's attitude. True that there are turns of fortune and they determine our life. But efforts can change the direction of the wind. Will can move mountains. Man should keep on with his efforts; he should not succuum or surrender but should keep fighting on — 'if winter comes can spring be far-behind' — so sang the poet Shelley Faith in oneself; in one's capacities and capabilities can turn the tide. Nothing is impossible for a man who possesses self-confidence and self-reliance. Misfortunes, if they come, should be treated as test times, they test your endurance, your forbearance, your fortitude and the dusk always turns into the dawn. If one sits holding his head that there is all darkness, whither to go, let him take steps forward and there would be light at the end of the tunnel. Man can make or mar one's life — fate and fortune are there but nothing is impossible to be achieved for a man of a strong will. Man is the maker of his fate and God also helps those who help themselves. There are trials and tests — God presents them but he also rewards them with results which results are won by one's own efforts. Man makes his fate — not fate the man.

❑ ❑ ❑

25. ALL THAT GLITTERS IS NOT GOLD

Appearances, sometimes are very deceptive. Particularly in the world as it is today, things are put up in a very attractive manner to attract people, and people also get attracted but intrinsically things do not happen to be what they look to be. Only recently a survey was published in the newspapers that very finely made gold ornaments which were put up as of 22 carat value were actually of 16 carat value. This is not only about ornaments. Even clothes or cloth material also deludes. But so far things are concerned it is all right. People discover the reality and may give up their use. But very much more deceptive are people with whom we come in contact. Very elegantly dressed, with an attractive personality, behaving in a very courteous manner and soon would befriend you. But it would be found that he is the worst crook who defrauds you of all your money or even go to the extent of taking your life or kidnap your child for ransom. Such cases get reported everyday in the papers. There was a great crook by the name of Natwar Lal whose exploits became proverbial. He indulged in such deceitful, even murderous exploits, enticed so many women, married them for their money and then disappeared in thin air. One needs to be very cautious in dealing with things and men. The world is full of false appearances and their glitter would appear as like gold but they would be dross like lead.

❑ ❑ ❑

WRITING LETTERS, APPLICATIONS AND INVITATIONS

WRITING LETTERS, APPLICATIONS AND INVITATIONS

Letters are of different sorts so are the applications. There are personal letters, there are business letters — there are letters written to members of the family and there are letters written to friends. Then there are letters written neither to members of the family nor to the friends but to people whom one distantly knows and with whom one has a formal relationship and one is writing the letter in some formal matter seeking some favour or some particular work to be done or to be got done.

All these letters have to have a different kind of content and style. Even their language would vary one from the other so would be their appellations and conclusions. One should only know their difference from examples and these examples are being given here.

Business letters are most formal and should be short and to the point — only dealing with the point of the business or the order to be placed or the contract to be entered into or some deal to be finalised.

Such letters have no personal touch.

Similarly applications are also of different types. There are applications written to the principal for leave or for getting books issued to you from the library in a number more than those allowed under rules; you may be sending an application for a post or applying to the

S.D.O. telephones for a telephone connection or to the Corporation for getting the drains of your locality cleaned or the road to be repaired.

How would you address these applications; how and where would you mention your address, where would you put the date of the application and where the subject-matter, all these would form an important part of the application and has a particular defined format how you would draft it.

The examples given herein would explain to you the correct form and the correct method and would serve as your guidance.

SPECIMEN LETTERS

PERSONAL LETTERS — (To direct relations)

On receiving a Birthday Gift

50, Jubilee Hostel
Allahabad University
Allahabad

December 2, 20___

Respected Papa,

I was so delighted to receive your telegraphic moneyorder for Rs. 200/- as a Birthday gift to me. You have always remembered to send me something as a Birthday gift. This time when I did not get any even till two days before my birthday, I was feeling a little disturbed — how and why I have not received anything from you. I felt that either you had gone out on tour or got otherwise busy and just missed to send anything but then this amount received through a telegraphic money order gave me such a delight. I always need your blessings more than anything and the moneyorder contained your blessings too in the message. How much I value them and feel so happy to receive them.

I shall use this valuable amount in throwing out a party to four of my dear friends here in the hostel, who would also feel so happy to know about this gift. I, of course, could not have afforded to extend this party without this money. Once again I crave your blessings and of Mama too. Kindly convey my regards her too.

May I tell you that I would be saving Rs. 50 out of this amount to purchase a nice pen which I had seen only yesterday at a shop and had very much liked it. This would remain with me as a valued gift for my examinations in which I shall use this. I wish I could really do well at the examination to pay due honour to this gift from you as I shall take it.

I am studying hard and all my arrangements in the hostel are fine. The mess is serving reasonably good food and I keep supplementing it with the snacks that Mama had packed up for me when I left last after the vacations.

I shall keep writing to you. Do please keep writing back to me. My love to dear Ritu.

With respectful regards,

Yours affectionately,

Rahul

To an elder brother asking for his guidance how to prepare for the competitive examination.

50, Jubilee Hostel
Allahabad University,
Allahabad

March 4, 20___

My dear Bhaiyya,

I hope you are doing well along with Bhabhi and dear Pankaj and Pinki.

I was glad to know of your promotion and your posting to Delhi. How happy do I feel about all that you have achieved — and all through your hard labour and honest work.

As per your advice I have decided to take the Civil Services Examination this very year, though the time for preparations is not much. I shall be finishing my examinations on the 18th of this month and then put in all effort in preparing for the Prelims. I shall be offering Political Science as one of the subjects as advised by you. With your experience, your advice is what I value most. I would now like you to send me a detailed advice how I should plan my preparations. What should I be consulting for my General Studies and how I should plan the preparations of this subject, which has a vast course? In Political Science also a planned study is called for — that had been your subject too, though, of course, there have been a lot many changes since you took the examination. Still the pattern of preparation remains the same and you can best guide about it.

I keep too busy these days with my examinations, hence I am not able to write a more detailed letter.

My preparations for the present examinations are going on well and all other things are as usual and normal.

I shall eagerly await your reply. With regards to you and to Bhabhi and love to Pankaj and Pinki.

Yours affectionately,
Rahul

❑ ❑ ❑

A letter to mother in wanting her to postpone fixing up his marriage.

27, G.N. Hostel
Allahabad University
Allahabad

January 20, 20___

My dear Mamma,

It was really a surprise to receive a letter from you, as perhaps, this is the first one that I have received during these last six months that I am here. But then I felt so good that you wrote it.

Only what you write is rather disturbing. I am yet to get my appointment letter, though I have finally made it to the Bank P.O. Competition. After I get the appointment letter, I shall be joining my training course which will last for three months, only thereafter shall I get my posting orders. Everything, therefore, is all so early and so premature. Let me at least settle down in my new job and adjust myself in it, before I can think of marriage and all that.

So why do you propose to be in such a haste about it. I am just 24 years—not getting two late for marriage. Do pray, consider my point too. I know of your anxiety and your concern for me, I do know that you have chosen a girl whom you have liked. Believe me, I shall go by your choice — I know, one whom you choose would be the best for me but then, it would be no harm waiting at least for a year more. The girl would also have completed her computer course by that time — that would be so good. She also, then, can take up a job if she wants to and I am sure you do not mind that too.

You want me to come down and meet the girl myself. That I would do, if you so want it. But please, mamma do not hurry for the marriage — that I would really and earnestly pray.

I have ever respected your wishes — they have been commands for me and in this matter also I shall abide by your choice — but then give me, please, just one year to mentally settle down in my new job and in my new environments. Hope you would appreciate my point and the girl's parents would also understand my stand.

Please tell Papa about it. I am not writing to him for the present, rather would talk to him when I come there. I shall be reaching there on February 1. During this period I have to wind up my affairs here before I finally leave the hostel.

Pray, do not take any, offence on what I am writing. Give it a cool consideration. I am all for your Wishes — You are my loving mom.

My regards to Papa and love to dear Anshu.

Your affectionately,

Dinkar

Letter to a friend congratulating him on his marriage.

27, G.N. Hostel
Allahabad University
Allahabad

January 20, 20___

Oh Hi, dear Shanu,

I really have felt thrilled to learn that you are getting married. How so quietly have you settled the whole matter without even giving me a hint about it earlier. However, that's going to be wonderful — I shall be there with you two days in advance. We shall all have so much of fun. It's going to be a great day for you and really a great day for all of us. You are getting married. Whom should I congratulate — You or your would be. Both deserve my heartiest good wishes. She is such a fortunate being to be getting such an eligible groom. It seems with you — it never rains but pours. You are on such a nice job recently got and now you are getting a nice companion too to share your achievements — this is an added achievement too.

So once again my congratulations and best wishes.

I look forward for the nice day.

All the best — Very best.

Yours as ever
Chum
Vijay

❑ ❑ ❑

Letter to the daughter who has got settled in a foreign land and has got selected on a high-profile job.

15, Ashok Nagar
Varanasi

October 4, 20___

Dear Dear Gunji,

It has really been a wonderful news from you. I got your letter just yesterday and have felt so happy about it. It has just been eight months that you have been there and within this short period you have made such a wonderful achievement. How proud do I feel to learn that out of 16 candidates drawn from all foreign countries, the selection board found you the best and the most suitable for this high job. It speaks so much of your calibre and your confidence. It is really very responsible position on which you would be working with nearly a dozen people, mostly foreigners, working under you.

Shushant should be really-feeling great about your achievement. Please convey my blessings to him too and congratulations as well. You have ably matched him in your attainments.

So how is everything else with you; with your new house and your new car. Everything is coming up so quickly in close succession.

Do please write back to me more details about the process of your selection as also how you are finding life there. No problems — I suppose?

Let me see when I would get the chance of being with you to personally share your achievements.

With lots of love to both of you.

Your affectionately,
Papa

Letter to a friend who has sent me his latest book published recently, for a review.

E2/12 Ashiana Colony
Aishbagh
Lucknow

March 2, 20___

Dear Saurab,

I have received your letter along with which you have sent me you latest book which has just recently come out.

I did not find time to go through the entire book as I had been keeping busy with some of my own projects. But then I have turned over its pages and have found the very beginning quite interesting. You have taken up rather a controversial subject on which you have chosen to pen your thoughts. Such subjects, of course, need a very thorough study and research and from the first three chapters that I have gone through, I find that you have worked hard to collect the material.

But may I point out that I am not in full agreement with some of the conclusions that you have drawn. Facts of history need to be recorded with an unbiased view point while your views appear to have a pre-conceived bias. But whatever it is, you have put up your point in a very convincing and cogent manner — the language and expressions are very facile.

I would let you have a detailed review of the entire book after going through it. It may take me sometime, say a couple of months as I have some of my own work to be completed.

You would not mind this delay, I am sure.

Keep up with your researches and come out with more authentic details — that is my advice and wish. Your efforts are promising.

Best wishes —

Your sincerely,
Sushil Kumar

Dr. Saurabh Chandra
A 15, Staff Quarters
Delhi University
Delhi

❑ ❑ ❑

A letter to you neighbour asking him to keep his dog in chain.

16 Lajpat Nagar
New Delhi

November 6, 20___

Dear Shri Charan

This is just to inform you that only yesterday while I went for a walk in the morning I found your dog straying on road and barked at me rather ferociously. If I had not my stick with me with which I warded him off, he could even have bitten me. That is what I felt.

I would, therefore, like you please to keep your dog properly chained or when brought out there should be some one to attend on it, otherwise it could be dangerous.

Please do not mind my pointing this out to you, but I thought it proper to do so.

Thanks

Your faithfully,
Mohan Singh

Sir Devi Charan
21, Lajpat Nagar
New Delhi

❑ ❑ ❑

A letter to a newspaper, complaining about the nuisance of loudspeakers in the locality blaring out when the Board's Examinations are on.

To,

The Editor
The Hindustan Times
Kasturba Gandhi Marg
New Delhi

Dear Sir,

It is through the columns of your esteemed daily that I wish to draw the attention of the civic authorities about the great nuisance that the loudspeakers blaring out 'Bhajans' and 'Kirtans' in the name of Puja in my locality. Our Board examinations are on and this causes a great disturbance in our studies. I approached the organizers with my complaint but they would not take any notice of it. Such a public nuisance is rather unpardonable and I have taken recourse to the columns of your esteemed

'Daily' to bring this to the notice of the concerned authorities for an immediate action.

Thanking you,

Yours faithfully,
Subhash Sharma

15, Laxmi Nagar
Rajpura
New Delhi
March, 2, 20___

❐ ❐ ❐

Letter to the Editor, The Times of India bringing to the notice of the Transport authorities to change the route of buses for the convenience of commuters.

To,

The Editor,
The Times of India
New Delhi

Dear Sir,

Through the columns of your esteemed daily, I would like to draw the attention of the Transport authorities of Delhi, to the great inconvenience that daily commuters have to face in reaching their work-place or offices in time due to lack of timely bus service. With a little diversion of Bus Nos.15 and 18 plying between Shaktinagar and Shahadra to Vaishali, the daily commuters would be greatly convenienced while there would be no inconvenience caused to the commuters and passengers as at present using them. The Delhi Transport Authorities would do well to please consider this suggestion at the earliest.

Thanking you,

Yours faithfully
Jasbir Singh

14, Sector B, Vaishali
New Delhi
September 12, 20___

❑ ❑ ❑

Letter to the newly elected Councillor of your ward to the civic problems that face your locality.

77, Dilkusha Garden
Civil Lines
Bareilly

March 4, 20___

Dear Shri Chaudhary,

I wonder if you would recollect that during your election I was not just your supporter but a campaigner in your favour too.

As so actively engaged in campaigning for you, had tried to convince people of this locality that if you got elected all our problems would get solved.

But I am sorry to have to point out that ever since you got elected people of the colony keep asking me, what has happened to all those promises.

You had yourself addressed meetings and assured the residents that all their civic problems would get solved within a month. Now it is more than three months that you got elected. The drains remain choked, the approach road to the colony has pot holes which makes commuting so risky and difficult, the tube lights on the poles remain unlighted. These are some of the basic amenities that the residents expected to have been set right.

I am pointing out to you all of these problems and would like you please to have them set right at the earliest.

I feel so embrassed when people ask me what has happened to our councillor.

You would do well to pay a personal visit to the colony and take early steps to get all these problems solved.

Thanks,

Your sincerely,
J.C. Sharma

Sri S.L. Chaudhary
Councillor
Sector B, Garden House
Dilkusha Gardens,
Civil Lines, Bareilly

❑ ❑ ❑

Letter to a friend inviting him to join you at a trip to Nainital.

23, Purana Kila
Sadar Bazar
Lucknow

May 2, 20___

Dear dear Chintoo,

Have not heard from you for long. How is it? You seem to have got all lost. Should I send some 'Lost and

Found', notice to the newspaper? Of course, not that. Must be keeping busy after your affairs at home since your father got unwell. You did inform me on phone that day that he was now well. It was just when you had reached home — two months back. Hope that he would now be perfectly well.

It was just two days back that Shyam and Rajneesh were with me. They have planned a short week-long trip to Nainital. They have already made arrangements of stay etc. there. They are keen that you also joined in this trip. That would be a good fun — all of us together for a week. We would do some hiking, some sight seeing around Nainital — there are places of picnic which are enjoyable. Let me know immediately — rather phone up and confirm. I am sure you would — won't you ? It would really be nice company if you are also there.

I shall so eagerly await your message.

Convey my regards to your Papa and Mummy.

All the best —

Yours as ever
Ashish

BUSINESS LETTERS

An order for ceiling fans for the school

From,

Manager
Adarsh Public School
Naya Bazar,
Gautam Nagar

To,

Iron Products
Latouche Road
Lucknow

March 4, 20___

Subject : Order for 30 (thirty) Crompton Ceiling Fans — 56″

Dear Sir,

As per our earlier communications on the subject, we have approved your quotation and the conditions of payment.

Please supply 30 (thirty) Crompton Ceiling fans of 56″ size at the earliest.

Please ensure that they are properly and securely packed.

The amount as required by you in advance is being sent herewith through a Bank Draft.

Thanking you,

Yours faithfully,
(G.S. Chowdhary)
Manager

❒ ❒ ❒

An order of books for the Library.

From,

Manager
Modern School
Kali Than, Bijnore

To,

Universal Book Depot
Hazratganj, Lucknow

June 12, 20___

Subject : Order for books for the School Library

Dear Sir,

Please find herewith the list of books selected by us from out of the catalogue sent by you. The list is enclosed herewith.

You would please supply the books and send on the bill along with them.

The payment would be made to you within a month.

Please ensure that you would give to the institution 20% discount over the printed price of the books, which condition you have already agreed to.

An early delivery of the books would be appreciated.

Thanking you,

Your faithfully,
(K.S. Sharma)
Manager

APPLICATIONS

From,

Dr. C.S. Naidu
P.G.T. Teacher
G.B. Inter College
Gurgaon

To,

The Manager
Holy Cross Inter College
Barakhambha Road, New Delhi

Subject : Application for the post of the Principal

Dear Sir,

With reference to the advertisement appearing in the 'The Times of India' New Delhi, dated April 2, 20___ for the post of the Principal of your college. I herewith submit my application for the same.

I had a uniformly good academic record; have got a Ph.D. Degree and have a total eighteen years experience as a P.G.T. Teacher at the above noted college.

Along with the teaching of my subject — Chemistry — I have been in charge of the different extra curricular activities of the college and have been helping the administration of the school in different capacities.

The result at the Board's examination in my subject has never been below 92%.

For further details of my qualifications — academic and administrative — I am herewith enclosing my biodata.

If given a chance, I shall do my best to justify your selection.

Thanking you,

Yours faithfully,
(C.S. Naidu)

April 2, 20___

❒ ❒ ❒

Application for leave to the Principal for attending the marriage of a brother

To,

The Principal
J.T.C. School
Model Town
Delhi

Sir,

I humbly request you to kindly grant me leave for three days — January 15 to January 17, 20___, to attend the marriage of my elder brother. The 'Barat' is going to Gwalior on the morning of January 15 and returning by the evening of January 16. On January 17, would be the reception party.

Thanking you,

Yours obediently,
Subhas Gupta
Class IX B

January 12, 20___

❒ ❒ ❒

Application to the Principal for books from the Library

To,

The Principal
Bal Bhawan School
Malviya Nagar
New Delhi

Sir,

I humbly bring this to your kind notice that while travelling by a bus, back from school day before, somebody lifted away my bag of books which I had kept close to my seat. The bus was awfully crowded.

The examinations are only a month after. I come from a very poor family and my father will not be able to afford purchasing all the books. I am feeling greatly disturbed.

I am making a very special request that books may be ordered to be issued to me from the library as a special case, otherwise I would lose my year which would be very hard on me.

I have always been securing a position among the first three in the class in all my classes.

My class teacher has testified to this fact and he has also recommended my application.

I shall feel greatly obliged if this favour is granted to me.

Thanking you,

Yours obediently,
Iqbal Ahmad
Class VIII C

February 2, 20___

Application for a Telephone Connection

To,

The S.D.O.
(Telephones)
Lakshminagar, Shahadra
Delhi

Subject : Request for a telephone connection.

Dear Sir,

This is to bring to your kind notice that I had applied for a telephone connection three months back and has deposited the requisite fee etc. — a photocopy of the receipt is attached herewith.

My mother keeps unwell and in the event of any emergency, I would find myself in a great difficulty. There is no PCO booth also anywhere nearby.

I had already met you personally in this connection twice and you had told me that the telephone connection has been sanctioned and the telephone would be installed soon. But I have been waiting in vain for it now for a month and more. Considering the emergency of the situation as noted above, I would request you to please have the telephone installed at the earliest.

I will be highly obliged.

Thanking you,

Your faithfully
(Rakesh Mohan)
20, Lakshmi Nagar
(Gol para)
Shahadra

December 12, 20___

FORMAL INVITATION

A formal invitation for dinner

Mr. and Mrs. K.S. Lal

request the pleasure of the company of

Mr. and Mrs. B.N. Gupta

at

DINNER

on Thursday, December 4, 20___

at 8 p.m. at their residence.

December 1, 20___

❑ ❑ ❑

Reply of acceptance to this invitation

Mr. and Mrs. B.N. Gupta thank Mr. and Mrs. K.S. Lal for their kind invitation to Dinner on Thursday, December 4, 20___ at 8 p.m. They shall be glad to join at the Dinner.

December 2, 20___

❑ ❑ ❑

Reply of regret to accept the invitation.

Mr. and Mrs. B.N. Gupta thank Mr. and Mrs. K.S. Lal for their kind invitation to Dinner on Thursday, December 4, 20___ at 8 p.m., but regret their inability to accept due to a previously accepted invitation.

December 2, 20___

❑ ❑ ❑

Informal invitation

12, Raisina Road
New Delhi

January 1, 20___

Dear Kaushal,

I and my wife shall feel obliged if you and Mrs. Kaushal join us at dinner tomorrow, January 2, 20___ at 8 p.m. at our residence.

Yours sincerely
S. Kumar

❐ ❐ ❐

Reply of acceptance to this invitation

16 Barakhambha Road
New Delhi

January 2, 20___

Dear Kumar,

Thank you so much for the dinner today, January 2, 20___ at 8 p.m. at your residence.

I and my wife would be so glad to join you at dinner today at 8 p.m.

It would be a real pleasure.

Yours sincerely

R. Kaushal

❐ ❐ ❐

A letter to your friend describing your visit to a fair

15, Premnagar
Sapru Marg
Lucknow

November 12, 20___

Dear Amrit,

Not heard from you for pretty long. How is it? Why should you fall into a stupor so occasionally as about writing letters. I await it and feel happy in getting it. Anything new happening to you?

As for me, I keep enjoying my stay in Lucknow. Ever since I came here Samir takes care that he makes my stay enjoyable.

So he took me to the Diwalimela which was this time specially organized on the banks of the Gomti river. It was all such an enjoyable experience. The whole vast area was beautifully illuminated and stalls of all variety had been set up. The most enjoyable part was a magic show put up by a known magician of Lucknow. The tricks that he displayed were really amazing. He took the wrist watch of one from the audience and in the sight of all he threw it in the Gomti river, just on the bank of which the show was arranged. The man whose watch had been thrown looked so disturbed, but then the magician asked him to search his own pockets. He searched this and that and to his great surprise, it was there in the inner pocket of his coat. Every one felt so amazed. What this trick was nobody could know.

There were the acrobats performing hair-raising feats; there were group dancers from the rural areas presenting colourful dances. Then there were the boat races arranged by the boat club. There was so much of cheering, so much of clapping and it was a sight to see. The winners were presented with the silver replica of a boat.

But you know, I have a weakness for sweets. Ram Asrey, the noted sweet-seller of Lucknow had set up a beautifully arranged stall. I enjoyed his 'Kulfi' and Falooda — it was really a delicious delicacy.

Then there were the fire-works competition and it was a spectacle work seeing. Competitors had come from far and wide and that was a marvellous show.

The mela lasted for the whole night and can you imagine, we returned home practically when it was day break. The lights all along the banks of the river which has flickered and dazzled all might were now looked dimmer with the first rays of the sun rising on the horizon.

My visit to Lucknow this time has been really enjoyable.

How is every thing else with you ?

Do convey my regards to your papa and mummy.

Yours lovingly,

Rishabh

Letter to a friend describing a visit to Agra with the school trip.

'Sukh Sadan'
Purania Tal
Balrampur
October 5, 20___

Dear Dear Maneesh,

I am sorry as I could not write to you earlier. I had gone away on a four days long trip to Agra with the school tour.

Every year our school arranges a tour and this year it was proposed by students themselves that they had read a lot about Agra — its historical monuments — we should this time go and personally visit and see them. The proposal was readily accepted by the Principal. Arrangements began to be made in advance. Railway concession tickets were arranged from Gond to Agra Fort station and back. There were in all 80 students — boys as well as girls, accompanied by twelve teachers — gents and lady teachers and three servants.

Prior arrangements had been made to take us by two buses from Balrampur to Gonda. The train at Gonda was at 4.30 p.m. which was to reach Agra Fort station at 6.00 in the morning.

All the students had been asked to report at the school at 1 p.m. They had been asked to bring their dinner packets from home. Boys and girls were divided into groups and teachers were put in charge of their groups. Attendance was recorded, the luggage was loaded and just at 2 p.m. we left by buses for Gonda. There was a great enthusiasm among all. Guardians — mothers, fathers or brothers had come to see off their wards and with hilarity and slogans in favour of the school we left.

The train at Gonda was in time, teachers once again took the attendance of students under their charge. The train steamed in and we were all properly accommodated. Berths had been reserved. The luggage was properly arranged and the as train steamed off, there again were slogans raised in favour of our school 'Modern School, Zindabad'.

Passing through Lucknow junction, where students were asked to take out their dinner packets. Sweets brought by the school were served to them and night dawned and we all, chatted, held 'antakshiri', sang songs and by 10 p.m. all was quiet and every one went to sleep.

It was time to reach Agra; morning was dawning and how eager were we to be reaching the town that we had so much read about but had never seen — its great monuments — the Taj, the Fort, Fatehpur Sikri and the markets of Agra famous for 'Petha' and 'Dalmoth'.

The train reached on time. Arrangements had already been made. There were buses ready to receive us and take us to the Dharmashala where arrangements for our stay had been pre-arranged. Everything was planned, everything was in order. It was a comfortable accommodation and we were asked to get ready within two hours — washed and bathed. Breakfast, arranged by the school was served, the lunch packets were packed and there were buses to carry us around.

So at 8.30 a.m., we left the Dharmashala for our dream trip of Agra — its great monuments. We first went to Dayalbagh where a beautiful 'Samadhi' of the late 'guru' is being built. What a beautiful carving in marble, how symmetrical the designs, how life-like the blossoms and buds carved in marble. The whole structure was one full of art and beauty. It took us nearly two hours to go around this.

Then we were to leave for our dream-destination — The Taj. Leaving the bus at a distance, we had to walk down. As we stood at the main entrance — there before us stood that great wonder of the world — the dream in marble. The huge white dome, the tall minarets, the raised platform and the pathway leading to it — green grassy with flushing fountains. We had read in books of history about the Taj, but here was it in all its grandeur and glory. We just felt enchanted and wonder struck. We went round and round — could not feel satisfied — wanted to spend more and more time there. The river Yamuna quietly flowed beside it at the back. We spent nearly four hours there. The packets of our lunch were consumed — this satisfied our hunger but our eyes longed to keep looking on and on at the magnificence of the huge dome and the intricate workmanship. We could feel why people all across the world come up to witness this marvel of marvels.

Evening was desending and it was getting time for us to leave. With much reluctance we did leave casting the last lingering look at the Taj.

Now was our plan to go through the famous market of Agra, the Kinari Bazar. The buses had been required to park themselves on the other end of the market.

The Kinari Bazar of Agra is also a marvel in its own way. A narrow street runs all through and on both its flanks are shops which sell from a needle to anything. Shoes are Agra's famous product and there are wholesale markets all over — in the lanes and bye-lanes.

And then the huge mounds of 'Petha' and 'Dalmoth' — really a treat to the eye and an attraction to the tongue — on every corner and then the sizzling 'Chat' and the greasing Desi Ghee Halwa. Agra market is full of such delicacies.

Back to the Dharmashala by the evening, we had our dinner served by the Dharmashala Dhaba — a reasonably tasty one, which our Principal had pre-ordered for us.

Next morning, again an early breakfast of 'Kachori' and Jalebi and cups of tea with packed lunch packets, we headed to the Agra Fort — a huge structure built in red-stone. The inside of it — there was a guide taking us all around — the Dewan-e-Aam; the Dewan-e-Khas the Zanan Khana, and so many other parts — tell the story of Mughal glory. But it was a touching point from where the once emperor Shahjahan imprisoned by his son, was permitted by his son Aurangjeb to have a look at Taj Mahal — the mausoleum of his beloved queen Mumtaj Mahal. The forenoon was thus spent and in the afternoon we went to Sikandra, the tomb of Akbar — some eight kilometres away from Agra. This was also a well-maintained huge structure with green lawns in front. We had our lunch packets which served us the day's food. Back to Dharmashala; a quick dinner at the 'dhaba' and then the night's rest after the hectic day schedule.

Next morning again, the same routine — an early bath and a good breakfast and packets of packed lunch, we headed towards the last of our sight-seeing schedule — Fatehpur Sikri — some thirty kilometres away from Agra which Akbar had specially built to be his capital city but never permanently shifted to it. Its main gate is a huge one — called the Buland Darwaza —really 'Buland' — which means 'huge' in structure. Again a guide took us around. It is a widely spread huge red-stone palace. Just as we entered the inside campus, we were guided to the Dargah of Salim Chisti — the Saint whom Akbar greatly revered. Hindus and muslims — all visitors — visit it and it is said about it that what one asks for is granted. I also prayed there — and what should I have asked for — just that I get a good first division at my Board's examination and may do well in life. It was a huge campus — the various parts, the various places for queens — Akbar had a number of them — the 'sheesh mahal' — all with pieces of glass studded all over.

We were to catch the train for our return journey from Agra at 6.00 in the evening and the Fatehpur Sikri was our last item for the day. By afternoon, we had finished our going around. What I wondered was how such a huge structure with such massive stone blocks could be built then when there were no cranes, no means of modern transportation. But then that was that and Fatehpur Sikri also appeared as a marvel of architecture and that it was.

The buses carried us straight to the railway station. The train started from Agra, straight for Gonda — a metre — gauge one. We were really tired after the whole day's wanderings. We occupied our reserved berths. Snacks that had been brought from Balrampur arranged by the school, were served. We ate and talked and laughed and played within the compartment. The sun set in the west and darkness began to descend and so was sleep descending on us. It was to be an overnight journey which passed off well. Back to Gonda in the morning again, the bus journey from there to Balrampur and back to the school campus where our people were there to receive us.

Such an enjoyable and unforgettable experience — a lifetime experience indeed.

You were not with us, but I hope you would have enjoyed the trip through your imagination — all that I have told you about through this letter. The letter has become lengthy indeed, but how could I not tell you all and everything about it. You are a dear friend to me indeed.

My best regards to your papa and ma.

Yours loving friend,

Abhai

Write a letter to your father telling him how you have suffered an accident and need money immediately for treatment.

Sherwood School
Hostel
Nainital
September 2, 20___

Respected Papa,

I got your last letter a few days back and should have written to you earlier. But it so happened that while coming down from the school in the evening along with my friends, I slipped over the stony pathway. I fell on my left and felt a great pain. My friends helped me to get up but then the pain in the shoulder was great. My friends took me back to the hostel, informed the house-master who immediately took me to the hostel dispensary. The doctor there examined the shoulder, he wanted to move it but I felt a great pain doing it. He advised the house-master to inform the Principal and take me to the Civil hospital. The Principal phoned up the Surgeon at the Civil Hospital. Two of my friends and the house-master took me to the hospital. I was having a terrible pain. The surgeon advised an X-ray and it was discovered that I had suffered a simple fracture in the shoulder. The Surgeon had given me some medicines and has plastered the shoulder. That has given me some relief. The surgeon says that the plaster will have to be there for three weeks, but I am required to keep taking some medicines.

Please do not get unduly disturbed and anxious. Tell mama also please, not to get unduly worried. The doctor says that there is nothing that serious. The house-master and my friends keep helping me and that gives me a great relief. I shall keep on informing you. Do not please get that worried to rush to Nainital — I am all right and hope to get well soon. My right hand is working all right so I can attend classes and my studies are not suffering.

Just because, the doctor wants me to keep taking some medicines etc. I do need some money at the moment which kindly arrange to send as soon as possible.

Everything else is all right with me. Nothing that much to worry at all. Mama gets upset too soon — So please tell her that I shall come down for some days as soon as the plaster is removed and the doctor allows me to travel.

It was good that the fracture is just a simple one — nothing that serious at all — let me reassure you.

The Principal may also be writing to you — that's what he told me.

Once again, don't worry at all.

My regards to you and to Mama. How is Vinni doing at her studies. My love to her.

Your loving son,
Sukant

❒❒❒

Letter to a neighbour whose bitch has given birth to four pups out of which one is requested to be given.

D 41, Subhas Marg
Sivpuri (M.P.)

December 2, 20___

Dear Uncle,

Your bitch — Softy — has given birth to four pups — that is so nice. I have seen them and I have very much liked the one which is all white. It looks so cute. I so much wished to have one as a pet and I would very much like if you may give me this one.

I would feel obliged if you could spare it for me and have not promised it to anyone else.

Hope you would.

My regards to you,

Yours sincerely,

Ajit

❑ ❑ ❑

Letter to a mother describing how you are enjoying holidays at your Mama's residence.

54, Civil Lines,
Dehradun

May 2, 20___

My dear Mom,

I am having such a nice time at Mama's place. I am really enjoying my holidays.

Mama is planning to take us all to Mussoorie for a week. He has some official work to attend to, some meetings etc. there and Vivek, Varun and I will have good time there. Mami is also coming with us. It was a couple of years back that I had gone to Mussoorie with you and Papa, then I could not go around so much as I had got laid up with fever.

So this time one week at Mussoorie would be a good time. We plan to visit the Kempti falls, and to go by the ropeway to Lal diggi. I would this time purchase a nice jacket for myself. Let me know what I may bring for you and for Veena.

Mama has made good arrangements for our stay and it would be so much fun and frolic — a real holiday for a week there.

After my return from there, I shall let you know when I should be reaching Roorkee. My regards to Papa and to you and love to Veena.

Yours loving son,

Vijai

❑ ❑ ❑

A letter to father about the course that is proposed to be followed after Intermediate.

Room No. 10,
Subhas Hostel
Bharti College
Meerut
January 8, 20___

Respected Papa,

I arrived here after the winter vacations and am doing well. Arrangements in the hostel have been improved. The mess runs regularly and the new contractor is serving reasonably good food. The previous one was really mismanaging the whole affair. Proper food — that is the most important thing. Of course Mama has packed so many packets of snacks and sweets. My friends in the hostel also shared them with me and enjoyed them so much.

Now my final examinations are just two month's hence and I have started my regular studies in right earnest. But, Papa, is it so necessary that I should go in for Engineering? You, of course, want me to do so. But, somehow I am not so much interested in that course of study. I would rather want to break some new ground and go in for a course in Journalism. There is a lot of scope in that and there are innovative approaches that open up in that field. I have been thinking a lot about this and would like to complete for the entrance examination for the Bachelor's course in Journalism at the JNU or even at the Delhi University. The department of journalism is an upcoming department and if one does well, one can join any newspaper or even a T.V. channel. There would be scope in coming in contact with so many people — high — profile people in all branches. And after working here in India for a few years there can be quite a chance of going out to a foreign country. There are a lot many Universities offering scholarships and if I do well here, I can easily try for one such scholarship.

Kindly let me have your valued and well-considered opinion on the issue. Engineering is just a hackneyed line — nothing so very much innovative while I want to do something new, something which normally students do not go in for. Opportunities there are — of course — it needs an interest and command on language and confidence in oneself. That way, I feel qualified in every way to go in for this line.

I would be eagerly awaiting your reply on this matter.

My regards to you and to Mom.

Yours affectionately,

Sumit

A letter to a friend describing a visit to a library.

27, Ganga Hostel
Jubilee College
New Delhi

April 10, 20___

Dear Nishi,

I am writing to you April 10, 2001 after quite a long lapse of time.

Actually my final examinations were over just a week back, but I am staying in the hostel for some more time. I am keen to explore possibilities for admission in JNU in the Department of International affairs. There is an entrance examination held for this course and I want to prepare for this which can be possible only by being here for sometime.

In the same connection to consult some latest books and magazines I went to the American library in Mandi House. I had never been to this library before but had heard a lot about it.

I found the Library fully air-conditioned and therefore, an ideal place for serious study. Moreover, the general atmosphere of the library was so good — very cosy chairs, very quiet no noise. On one side of the entrance was a pleasing array of magazines and periodicals. To the right were shelves of books with a placard 'New Arrivals'. The new arrivals were mostly dealing with political science and economics subjects — it was actually such books on such subjects that I was keen to consult.

The Librarian sat in one of her cubicles while there was staff ready to offer you guidance and help. They seem to be quite knowledgeable and I took full advantage from their guidance in getting the right material that I was looking for.

I spent full four hours in the library, made copious notes and now intend visiting this library at least for full one week.

I hope you would'nt have felt bored with all that I have been writing in this letter — nothing have I said about what interests you — any new picture or any new cultural programme.

Better that I would meet you soon after this week and then shall talk a lot about so many things.

Bye for the present. Hope all well with you,

Yours lovingly,

Sushama

❑ ❑ ❑

A letter to a friend describing a visit to Nainital.

Burlington Hotel
Uphill Resort
Nainital
June 12, 20___

Dear Manisha,

I have come to Nainital with my parents to spend a week of holiday here. After the whole year of the busy and hectic schedule at the school during the year and my final High School Examinations being over, this trip seems to be a real relief. One needs to get out of the rut and one feels like doing so. So this trip is serving me dual purpose — a visit to a hillstation which I had not visited earlier and then a relief from the entire year's pressing programme of studies.

Manisha, as I have come here for the first time, everything seems so enjoyable. Particularly from the intense heat of the plains, it is a pleasant sensation — to be enjoying winters in summers. The mountain scenery is delightful. As one stands out in the campus of the hotel in which we are staying, one sees a variegated panorama of nature. The sloping mountains are all covered with pine trees — rising high at if touching the sky. A very novel phenomena is when clouds come hovering over the hills and even float into our room in the hotel from this door and that window. Never did I find clouds to be with us and we with the clouds. Our hotel stands on a height and is on the top of a hill. So the entire scene is all clear and unobstructed. I make it a point to get up from bed early in the morning as it is a delight to watch the sun-rise. So is the sight of the sunset. The glowing horizon presents a beautiful spectacle.

You can never be sure of the weather here. At one moment it is sunshine and just the other moment, clouds gather over the sky and it starts drizzling.

The wide-spread area down below is what they call 'flats' — a spacious plain field. Hockey matches are played on it, then there are so many stalls of eatables — 'chat' and snacks and 'fast-food' joints. The Naina Devi temple is also at one end of the flats.

The lake of Nainital is an attraction in itself. We went across in boats — that is also a unique experience.

Would you believe, I along with my parents and some others who have grown friendly, we climbed up the highest peak called the China peak. It was a strenuous climb. But we could do it. Of course, on our return down we were dead tired.

So it is, I thought I should share my experiences with you — you who have always been my dear chum with whom I can share all experiences and all thoughts.

Do write back but to my home address as we are here just for a week.

My regards to your daddy and mummy.

Yours loving

Chum

Shalini

❑ ❑ ❑

Letter to a brother describing a hostel function.

Room No. 12
Modern School Hostel
Bara Khambha Road
New Delhi

My dear Bhaiyya,

I should have written to you earlier as you must have been awaiting my letter. Actually here the hostellers elected me the Secretary of the Social Club. They wanted a get-together party to be arranged as the session was closing. So I got busy arranging that. Of course, it was a pool-party, each one contributed to it. On the spacious lawns of the hostel, we arranged this party. It was still another novel experience. We were required to do the cooking ourselves — only Sweets were got from the Bengali Market. I had to arrange for the gas cylinders, the cooking utensils and the other cooking gadgets. But than we did it, and did it so well. There were items like potato cutlets, 'pakoris', and sandwitches and, of course, sauce and chilly-sauce.

We had invited the Superintendent of the hostel as well as the Warden. Even they put their hand in cooking.

And after the eating and drinking of soft drinks was over, we held a singing competition. It was compulsory for each one to sing and each one sang — some came out to be really good singers. Then was the 'quiz' competition. The warden gave away the prizes.

The whole function which had started around 5 p.m. went late into midnight — fun, frolic, story telling, jokes—all these items formed a part of the programme.

Hope you would appreciate that your younger brother can organize things. That is how it was.

Please write back. How is Bhabhi keeping ? Convey my regards to her and love to Shobhit and Shelley.

Yours affectionately,
Sushant

A letter to a sister who has missed a scholarship just by a few marks.

9, Vijainagar
Charbagh
Lucknow

April 9, 20___

My dear Diji,

I have often been writing to you, so, this letter is just one such. I keep enquiring about your studies, particularly because your academic achievements are a source of inspiration to me too.

You wrote to me in your last letter that you were preparing for the GMAT examination. If successful at that, it would qualify you to go abroad for higher studies. You, of course, did not inform me but I learnt from a letter from Papa that you missed this scholarship just by a few marks and are feeling distressed and depressed. Why should you feel so? There are chances again in future and with your dedication and devotion to achieve your aims you would quality the next time. That the sincerely wish and hope.

I have still many more years to go to reach your level of achievement. You have always been a source of inspiration to me and I keep wishing and trying that I should also do as well as you have done in your academic career.

Though, much too younger to lend you any advice, but then, Diji, do not lose heart. Struggles bear fruit — that what they say. So the next would be the best. You have to succeed. I offer you my sincere good wishes.

With lots of love and regards,

Your affectionate brothers
Kamal

❑ ❑ ❑

A letter to mother for a Birthday Gift.

E12/35, DLF City
Phase I
Gurgaon

March 20, 20___

My dear dear Mamma,

You would be surprised to receive this closed envelop from me. I could have told you about it, but I am writing this down to reassure myself.

March 27, is my Birthday. You have always given me wonderful gifts but now I do not want any more toys or anything of that sort.

You had given me 'The Children's Mahabharata' series. I have read them through and have known many things.

Now I would love to have the 'Children's Ramayana' as my Birthday Gift.

Don't you feel happy that I have begun to love reading books? So I shall await my Birthday Gift along with your blessings.

Papa would also like my choice.

Regards and love.

Yours loving child,
Utkarsh

About changing the timings of the library — application to the Principal.

To,

The Principal
Adarsh Vidyalaya,
Navnagar, Delhi.

Sir,

It is on behalf of all my classmates of class VIII that I am submitting this application.

Most respectfully I wish to submit that the college Library issues books only between 2 p.m. and 4 p.m. This is the time when our classes are on and we cannot make use of the books from the library.

This is to request you to kindly order the change in the timings of the library — let they be 9 a.m. to 10 a.m. and 3 p.m. to 4 p.m. during the winter season when the college starts at 10 a.m. and closes at 3 p.m. During the summer season the timings of the library can be 7 a.m. to 8 a.m. and 2 p.m. to 3 p.m.

These timings would be convenient to all the students of the school.

It is hoped that the request would be duly considered.

Thanking you,

Yours obediently,
Anurag Prakash
Class VIII B.

November 3, 20___

❑ ❑ ❑

Order for books to be sent by V.P.P.

To,

Sahitya Sadan
Laxmi Market,
Allahabad.

Dear Sir,

I am enclosing herewith a list of books which I urgently need for the preparation of my entrance examination to the Polytechnic after my High School Examination.

Please send on these books by V.P.P. at the address as given below.

Thanks,

Yours faithfully,
A.K. Sarm

44, Civil Lines
Sultanpur (U.P.)
March 4, 20___

❑❑❑

Application to the Health officer, Municipal Board, Barabanki for getting the drains in front of his house cleaned.

To,

The Health Officer
Municipal Board,
Barabanki.

Dear Sir,

We are at present in the midst of our Intermediate examination and it becomes so difficult to be studying at night due to the mosquito menace. This sudden rise in this menace is, as I think, due to the overflowing drains filled with all the garbage littered all around. It is becoming awful a menace and you would kindly appreciate it and order your sanitary department to take immediate steps to eradicate this menace.

An early action is requested and would be appreciated.

Thanking you,

Yours faithfully,

Akhilesh Chandra

House No. 42
K.D. Singh Babu Road
Barabanki

March 5, 20___

❑ ❑ ❑

An application to a Principal for permission for a Cricket match.

To,

The Principal
St. Francis School,
Lucknow.

Sir,

We, the members of the 'A' Cricket Team of our school — Red Hill School — want to play a friendly Cricket match with the 'A' cricket team of St. Francis School on Sunday, the 14th December at your School playground.

We would request you to kindly grant permission for the match as also for the use of your cricket ground.

Our application has duly been forwarded by our Principal.

Thanking you,

Yours obediently,

Abhishek Sharma

Captain 'A' Team (Cricket)

Red Hill School

December 10, 20___ Lucknow

❐❐❐

Application to the Principal for permission for a picnic trip .

To,

The Principal
Shanti Dham School,
Vishnupuri,
Varanasi.

Madam,

We, the girls of Class X plan to go out on a picnic to Sarnath for a day, on Sunday, October 12.

Madam Malini and Madam Sheela have agreed to accompany us and to guide us. Girls who have contributed towards this trip are 62.

We request you kindly to permit us to go for this picnic.

We would also request you to allow us to use the school bus for the trip. We shall pay for its fuel charges.

Madam Malini and Madam Sheela have recorded their consent on our application and have recommended the trip. It would be a picnic as well as a study of history.

We hope our request would be granted.

Yours obediently,
Girls of class X

October 9, 20___

❑ ❑ ❑

Application to the Principal complaining about the insanitary conditions in the school toilets.

To,

The Principal
St. John's Girls School,
Agra.

Madam,

We, through this application, want to bring to your kind notice how the toilets of the school remain very dirty and no antiseptic spraying is done in them.

This has been going on now for sometime and inspite of our telling the sweepress a number of times, things have not improved. It is causing insanitary conditions and can be very infectious.

This is to request you to issue necessary orders to the staff to put things right.

Thanking you,

Yours obediently,
Girls of the School

November 2, 20___

Monitors of classes have signed the application.

1. ....
2. ....
3. ....
4. ....
5. ....
6. ....
7. ....
8. ....
9. ....
10. ....

❑ ❑ ❑

Application for a Job.

The Commander
Para-Military Force
Cantonment
Agra

Subject : Recruitment of cadets to the force.

Sir,

With reference to the advertisement appearing in the newspapers of the recruitment of cadets to the para-military force under your kind command, I wish to present myself as a candidate.

The age requirement, educational qualifications and physical fitness standards aptly fit me for the selection.

1. My age on date is 18 years, I passed my High School examination last year from the U.P. Board of High School and Intermediate Education and was placed in the II division with distinction in mathematics.
2. My height is 5′8″.
3. I had been taking part in the games and sports of the school and have won several prizes.
4. I possess a robust physique.

If given a chance, I am prepared to undergo all physical tests and feel confident that I shall do well in them.

Further details on the prescribed proforma as required are submitted herewith.

Thanking you,

Yours faithfully,
Shanker Singh

55, Swedeshi Bima Nagar
Agra
September 12, 20__

❑ ❑ ❑

Application for Admission to a Computer course.

To,
The Director,
Crash Computer Course
Delhi.

Subject : Application for admission to the preliminary course in computers.

Dear Sir,

I came across your advertisement appearing in the newspapers that you are starting a short-term preliminary course in Computers at your institute for those who have passed the High School examination.

I passed my CBSE High School examination this year and have been placed in the I Division with 87% marks.

Before I join the Intermediate classes, I would like to utilise my vacations to benefit from the Computer Course Training that you have started as a preliminary course for High School passes. I already had computer as one of my subjects at the High School and that, perhaps, would help me still more to take benefit from this short-term course in computers that you have started.

I am prepared to be put to any test for admission to the course.

I would request you to consider me for selection to this course.

Thanking you,

Yours faithfully,

Amar Prakash

17, Sadar Bazar Road,

Delhi

May 2, 20___

❑ ❑ ❑

An invitation to a Birthday Party.

Dear Dear One
Come all and one
My Birthday Tenth
It'll be pleasant
Pizza Corner
Reach the Sooner
We'll have fun
We'll race and run
From five 'o' Clock
That's the time stock
Enough enjoyment
Full contentment
Vinay requesting
No dissenting
Come, Come, Come
All friends Come

From Vinay — Your friends
To All friends.

Application to S.H.O. Police about cycle thefts in the hostel.

To,

S.H.O.
Incharge,
Rajamandi Police Station,
Agra.

Subject : Recurring thefts of cycles from the hostel.

Dear Sir,

We, the hostellers of the Subhas Hostel of Agra High School, Agra, want to inform you that there have been recurring cases of thefts of cycles from the hostel for the last two months. We have already lodged three complaints of thefts but, we are sorry to find that no action has been taken and the cycles have not been recovered. There seems to be some gang operating in the area who keeps lurking for on opportunity. Surprisingly, even locked cycles have been lifted.

This is causing us a great loss as well as inconvenience. That these happenings are taking place in the area under your charge and no theft getting detected speaks against the laxity of your police personnel or, may be your lack of interest in the cases.

This is the last report that we are lodging with you and hope that an effective step would be taken in tracing out the cycles and in catching the culprits.

We have come personally to lodge this complaint and even if after this no action is taken at your end, we shall be obliged to approach the higher authorities.

The details of the cycles stolen — their make, their number, their design, everything has been recorded in the FIR filed earlier.

We earnestly hope for an early and effective action on your part.

Thanks

Yours faithfully,
Hostellers of Subhash Hostel
Agra High School,
Agra

December 10, 20___

A letter from a Class XII student to a friend on the crucial issue of the examination pressure resulting in suicides.

15, Shalimar Bagh
New Delhi
March 19, 20___

Dear Anshu,

You may find this letter of mine, rather unusual — unusual in the sense that it is not regarding any personal matter or about any proposal for a picnic that I am writing this.

Today's Hindustan Times brings a news which has greatly upset me and I want to share my feelings with you.

The news says that a young boy who was appearing at the class 12 examination could not cope with the dejection of not having measured up to his own expectations and thus 17 year old student hanged himself by a bedsheet from the ceiling fan of his room and committed suicide. This happened a week after he took his mathematics paper. Ever since March 6 examination, though outwardly calm, the boy was feeling severely disturbed. His father, an officer in the army, had taken a break only to be with him during his examination of the board. The boy had broached the topic of his disappointment to his father, who had liked any other father, gave him all consolation and tried to boost him up. Not a word of reproach was addressed to him. Still, this also could not console the boy and he committed the most dreadful deed of ending his life in this manner — a terrible shock and loss to the parents and to the family to lament for all their lives. A youngman of 17, in the prime of his youth, on the threshhold of his life, gives up in such a frustration. The news has been really disturbing me ever since I read it in the paper. I really feel a great sympathy for thc bereaved parents, but I really feel no sympathy for the boy, rather I feel a pity on his indiscretion and impetuous action.

What was that frustrating for him as to end his life ? He had a weak will, otherwise life offers to many chances, failures do not close all doors, life can be better lived by struggling and striving — not by giving up in this way. What did he get therefrom — he, of course, lost his life but never did he think what misery and agony was he leaving behind for his parents and family. Class XII was not the be-all and end-all of life. Worst for most, even if he had failed, he was just 17 years old — life lay long for him — more efforts, more endeavour could bring better results. Life is not given to be lived just as we want it to be — there can be ups and downs, there can be rise and falls — but go on, carry on, struggle on — that is my way of thinking. Don't think I am haranguing too many platitudes and high sounding ideals but I am saying what I really feel about such a giving up of life. We need to fight odds — that is how life has to be lived and not to get defeated so soon. Anything else lost can be gamed; an examination once failed can be passed but life once lost cannot be got back.

I hope you would also agree with what I say and feel. At least that is what my way of thinking is — may appear a little too mature at this immature age but it is from now that we have to begin seasoning our minds to prepare for life.

A point, of course, about these board examinations too. There are cases year after year reported of such suicides only due to frustrations. The system of these examinations needs also to learn something from these unfortunate incidents. Let there be a year long process of evaluation so that there is no such peer pressure at the eve or during the examination. The student could keep on coolly appearing at these periodical tests — answer-scripts may be evaluated at other centres — answer-scripts may be evaluated at other centres — there may be an exchange of evaluators from one school to another and that would eliminate the possibility or the apprehension of favour or disfavour. This system, if can be developed, can go a long way in eliminating the undue pressure put on students at the time of examination.

What do you think of this? It is not an innovative thinking on the part of a would be examinee? I have also to take the class XII examination next year but I keep cool and calm, remain regular with my studies and God willing, shall have no pressure to suffer from.

My faith in my thoughts would sand doubly reassured if you also endorse them.

I would so much like if you show this letter of mine to your Mom. She may also, perhaps, appreciate and endorse them.

Write back your views and reactions. I shall await your letter in reply rather eagerly.

Hope your studies are going on well. We, both have to face the ordeal of this examination next year — do it with all coolness and composure — take my advice in the matter my regards to your papa and mom.

Yours lovingly,

Abhilasha

PRECIS WRITING

PRECIS WRITING

'Brevity is the soul of wit', this has rightly been said. Brevity, precision, conciseness are the key-note of good prose writing. Be to the point, do not be discursive, do not indulge in digressions, do not try to be very figurative or ornamental is words or phrases — a direct thing directly said appeals more in prose, figures of speech, flowery descriptions, similes and metaphors are permitted in poetry but they are, in a way prohibited from good prose. It does not mean that prose has no scope for emotions or expressions which deeply express feelings but normally prose has its own limitations. There are words that ring into the ears — that also is good prose but precision is a better style, even ringing words can be put together in a little space. Elaborate and detailed description can be condensed in a few words; the meaning remains the same but the space is less.

'Precis'—the word comes from 'Precision'. Thus the word 'Precis' connotes its intent and purpose. Everything that has been said in lengthy descriptions is said in a few words but every idea, and every fact is brought within it. Nothing important or relevant is left out. That is the quality of a good 'Precis'.

Summary and Precis

'Precis' should not be mistaken as 'Summary'. A summary is a form in which the thought or description that was elaborately said or described is shortened in space and put down in a few words. There is no concern with what is the central idea of the larger passage or what is the sequence or connection of ideas one with the other — what is the importance of ideas. A summary just summarises and does nothing else. There are no specific rules that govern writing down a 'Summary'. Summary is only a shortened version of a lengthier passage in the same order or sequence of thought.

But while writing a 'Precis' great care has to be taken to fish out the Central idea of the larger passage — what is the point which the writer wants to strike at — what is the theme, the key note and how the other ideas are connected with the central idea — how they help to form a logical sequence and elaborate the central idea step by step. That is the most important part of the 'Art of Precis Writing'.

There are some 'do's' and 'don'ts' in precis writing — what the precis writer should do and what he should not do. So, here in under are given some of those rules of Precis Writing which have to be followed, otherwise if not followed, the whole exercise would cease to have the due merit and the Precis-Writer would suffer the loss in the form of low marks. The following are the guidelines of Precis Writing. Examples have also been given to give a correct idea of the observance of these rules — how to observe them and in what manner.

Follow these guidelines carefully and the Precis can be perfect in its form.

Rules of Precis Writing

(1) Read the given passage, of which precis has to be written, very carefully.

In the first reading try to understand what the passage deals with.

In the second reading try to find out the central idea of the passage.

It may sometimes be that the writer might have discussed the different aspects of the subject in the earlier part and in the conclusion would come to what he actually wants to say — the Central Idea.

For example the writer may describe the details about the various aspects of the educational system and in the end may come to say that our entire education system is in a disarray and needs overhauling. But this he might say at the end of the passage.

The precis writer will have to find this out, rather fish it out, and while beginning to write the precise, this point should be brought first and in the forefront.

So in the second reading it is the central idea which would be needed to be discovered and also an idea formed what other ideas are closely connected with the central idea — how on the basis of what facts and ideas the writer has come to the conclusion.

So a final and third reading will have to be given to connect the ideas with the central idea and the closest idea to it be number 2 and similarly ideas should be numbered 3, 4, 5. In order of their closeness to the central idea and a sequence of ideas in order of importance should be determined and marked and numbered.

Now it is that you are ready to write down the precis.

Therefore, precis writing has to be an exercise in concentration, understanding and logical development of ideas.

This the first and foremost step in precis writing.

(2) The precis has be written in your own language. The phrases, or the language formation of the original passage have not to be adopted as such; the idea contained in them has to have language which is your own. Never should the sentences and phrases be lifted as such from the original passage.

(3) The word length of the precis has roughly to be one-third of the original passage. You can even count the words of the original passage and record them down and then count the words of the precis and note that number down at the end of the precis.

This would give to the examiner the correct impression of your effort and your effort to follow this rule.

If in your first attempt you find the word limit exceeding, try to find out what you still can eliminate to reduce the length to the required limit.

This means that the first draft would be a part of your rough work which, after the final writing you would cross out. But care needs also to be taken that the precis does not become too short. That would also go against the spirit if precis writing.

(4) Special care will have to be taken that all the matter, all the points salient and important get included in the precis; nothing that is important is left out in the effort at condensing the structure of the precis.

(5) Examples, illustrations, comparisons, figures of speech — all have to be eliminated from the precis.

The language of the precis has to be direct, without embellishments, but at the same time the precis should not seem to have a telegraphic languages — disconnected sentences, ill-arranged clauses — rather the precis should read like a well-formed, well-constructed passage. Precis should read like an original passage.

Opinion should not be expressed even if the precis-writer holds some opinions for and against the subject matter of the original passage.

The precis-writer is just like a reporter and not a commentator.

Care has to be taken regarding the grammatical form of the language of the precis. Any mistakes of grammar or composition would, of course, stand penalised.

(6) Normally a precis should be just in one consolidated paragraph. (This rule may not be

that binding on the lengthy passages set for the Civil Services Examination).

But here we are concerned with the lower standard of the examinees.

(7) Precis has always to be written in the indirect narration, even if the original passage is in the direct narration — a speech or a personal expression of opinion on any subject. While writing down the precis, the direct narration shall have to be converted into indirect narration. Rules of this conversion from direct to indirect narration should scruplously be followed. The pronouns 'I', 'me' or 'my' or 'mine' should get changed to 'he', 'him', 'his' etc.

The precis can begin, with 'The Author says that ......' If at the end of the original passage, the name of the writer or the speaker has been given, the precis can begin with 'William Hazlitt says that......' or so on. or Jawaharlal Nehru in his speech says, ...' or Winston Churchill expresses his views ......'.

(8) A suitable title may be given to the precis, even if not asked for. But herein, great care has to be taken in choosing the title as the title should embody the central theme and the choice of the title would, at the very outset, give the impression that the central idea has rightly been caught. Thus the choice of the title becomes so crucial to create the first impression about your understanding of the passage and its central idea.

Some general hints in the process of condensing words —

For example :

(1) 'There were dogs, cats, hens, ducks, geese, and pigs, barking, squealing, mewing, quacking all over—

This can be compressed as _

'Different animals and birds were making various noises.......'

(2) 'Carpenters, blacksmiths, tailors, shoe-makers — all had assembled there......'

This can be shortened as —

'Artisans of various trades had gathered ......'.

(3) One-word substitutions need also to be learnt — (a long list of these would be given later).

For example :

(a) 'They arrived all at the same time' —

In precis it can be said —

They all arrived simultaneously.

(b) 'You are liable to be called upon to explain your conduct'.

This can be shortened as —

'You are answerable for your conduct'.

(c) 'You have many weaknesses — one of them being that you easily believe what people tell you and you do not verify the facts'.

This in a precis would be 'Your weakness is that you are too credulous'.

(4) Figurative expressions and language has to be avoided as —

'The ambition which we preach about and the success which we prepare for are very often nothing but a missing of a simple road; a troubled wandering among thorny byepaths and dark mountains'.

All these figuratives can be simply said as

'The ambition and success sought after take us away from the right and straight path and lead to difficulties.

(5) Still another example—

'And then Gandhi came. He was like a powerful current of fresh air that made us stretch ourselves and take deep breaths, like a beam of light that pierced the darkness and removed the scales from our eyes; like a whirlwind that upset many things but most of all the working of people's minds'.

A simple condensation of all this can be —

'And then Gandhi came. His was a powerful enlightening influence which changed people's thinking and made them progressive'.

An example how the central idea has been placed at the end when so many unnecessary and unneeded points have been talked about earlier—

'Finally, a word about what a national language, spoken, written and thought might do for the threatre of India. With the new awakening in social life, the need for the common tongue is being increasingly felt. Much work is being done to hammer out a common linguistic medium. The day when it is accepted will be a great day for the Indian theatre as it will be for all art in the country. But the theatre, because its life blood, is spoken word, will gain most.'

The writer wishes to say just this —

'A common spoken and written language would benefit the threatre in the country most as it depends upon the spoken word'.

Some Sample Examples of Precis Writing

EXAMPLE 1

The position that Indian women occupy today is very largely the result of a little more than a century of earnest endeavour on the part of social reformers, educationists and political leaders; for it was the 20th century that really ushered in an era of dynamic change and new concepts which fundamentally affected the status of women, giving to it a fresh dignity and importance. In India, because of her political subjection at the time, progressive movements had a political tinge and were the reflection of people's determination to throw off the shackles of bondage. The women's movement was no exception to the rule. Therefore, it was only when India gained her political freedom and emerged as an independent sovereign Republic, the women truly came into their own as equal partners with men. This principle of equality was incorporated in the objectives Resolution of Free India in 1947 and was later elaborated in the Constitution of the India Republic'. *(159 words)*

Precis

Title : *The Attainment of Equality of Indian Women*

Indian woman attained their rights of equality and dignity with men only after India got independence and equality of women became first a part of the objective Resolution of Free India and later a part of the Indian Constitution. In this achievement social reforms, educationists and political leaders played an important part.

EXAMPLE 2

College is a preparation for life and life is infinitely wider than work. Life is also leisure and thought and family relationship; it is a play and art and religion; it is sleep and walking and death itself. Not only life is wider than work, it is only thing that justifies work. If you absorb life into work, you find that there is nothing to work for. Work must always lead beyond itself to a life of the mind by which the fruits of work may be enjoyed. To work is to make a tool of oneself: and man should not only be a tool but also the craftsman behind the tool. All too often, the call of action are so insistent that one has no time for the repose and thought fullness that enter into the building up of an inner life: one comes to live altogether outside oneself. And there is the opportunity of education. College should fill, to some extent, the role of medieval monasteries in which man take a refuge — an escape and take an inventory of his vital resources away from the bustle of the world and determine his place in the general scheme of things. It is impossible to complete this task in college but it is possible to begin it. *(217 words)*

Precis

Title : *Man's Complete Life*

A college should be the preparation ground for man's complete life. Man's complete life does not only lie in work but also in the development of his personality. Work alone should not engage a man's life; it is the man behind the work whose development is more important and man should work towards that end too. College offers the ground for this development; it does not do the total work but it prepares the ground for that. (*77 words*)

EXAMPLE 3

One of the heaven's best gifts to man is humour, for it adds innocent pleasure to life, both in health and in sickness, and helps to promote good feelings among people in their daily intercourse with one another. Sydney Smith says, "Man should direct his ways by plain reason, and support his life by tasteless food; but God had given us wit and flavour, and brightness and laughter, and perfumes to enliven the days of man's pilgrimage and to charm his pained steps over the burning marl." Think for a moment what life would be if there were no humours or wit in the world, no laughter, no fun. Now. humour is not the same thing as wit; wit is concerned chiefly with words while humour deals rather with situations; a man may be witty and yet not possess humour. Humour is something much larger and profounder than wit. Nearly all our great writers have the gift of humour.

But like all pleasureable things of life, wit and humour have their dangers; and three of the commonest are those of being vulgar, unkind and profane. In other words, those who use these gifts of wit and humour must see that they do not hurt the feelings of other and must avoid jesting about sacred things. The only way in which you can acquire a right taste for what is good in the world of wit and humour is for you to read good examples and fortunately we have many in our literature. Shakespeare is a mine in himself and so is Dickens. *(263 words)*

Precis

Title : *The Place of Humour in Life*

Humour adds charm and pleasure to the social intercourse in life and relieves even the miseries of sickness. Life without humour would be barren. But humour and wit are not synonymous. Wit is with words, humour is with mind and situations. But great caution is required in using humour. It should not hurt anybody's feelings. Writers like Shakespeare and Dickens give good lessons in the use of humour. *(72 words)*

EXAMPLE 4

Success grows out of struggles to overcome difficulties. If there were no difficulties, there would be no success. If there were nothing to struggle for or compete for, there would be nothing achieved. It is, therefore, that men should be under the necessity of exerting themselves. In this necessity for exertion, we find the chief source of human advancement — the advancement of individuals as nations. It has led to most of the splendid mechanical inventions and improvements of the age. It has stimulated the ship-builder, the merchant, the manufacturers, the machinist, the tradesman, the skilled workman. In all departments of productive industry it has been the moving power. It has developed the resources of this and of other countries — the resources of the soil, and the character and qualities of the men who dwell upon it. It seems to be absolutely necessary for the purpose of stimulating the growth and culture of every individual. It is deeply rooted in man, leading him ever to seek after, and endeavour to realise, something better and higher than he has yet attained. (*177 words*)

Precis

Title : *Struggle leads the Success*

If there had been no struggle there would have been no success. To exert oneself provides the driving force for men to advance more and more. Most of the great inventions of the modern age are due to this urge to struggle and achieve. This urge is absolutely essential for both individuals and nations to realise higher and higher goals. (*59 words*)

EXAMPLE 5

Old age, it is said, disqualifies us from taking an active part in the great scenes of business. But in what scenes ? Let me ask if in those which require the strength and vivacity of youth. I really admit the charge, but are there no other — none which are peculiarly appropriate to the evening of life and which being executed by the powers of the mind are perfectly consistent with a less vigorous state of body? Nothing can be more void of foundation than to assert that old age necessarily disqualifies a man for the great affairs of the world. As well might it be affirmed that the pilot is totally useless and unengaged in the business of the ship because, while the rest of the crew are more actively employed in their respective departments, he sits quietly at the helm and directs its motion. If in the great scenes of business an old man cannot perform a part which requiies the force and energy of vigorous years, he cannot act none-the-less in a nobler and more important character. It is not by expertions of corporal strength and activity that the momentous affairs of state are conducted; it is by cool deliberation, by prudent counsel and by that authoritative influence which ever attends on public esteem-qualifications which are so far from being impaired that they are usually strengthened and improved by increase of years. (*237 words*)

Precis

Title : *Old Age will ever have its Importance*

Old age may be lacking in the physical strength and high spirits of the youth but this does not disqualify old age for the great affairs of the old. Cool thinking and sane advice born out of experience and an authoritative influence are the assets that belong to the old age and can always be a source of guidance in life and its affairs and momentous decisions may need the advice of experience — which still continues to be with age.

(*77 words*)

EXAMPLE 6

India is supposed to be a religious country above everything else. The spectacle of what is called religion in India and elsewhere had filled me with horror and I have frequently condemned it and wished to make a clean sweep of it. Almost always it seems to stand for blind belief and reaction, dogma, bigotry, superstition and the exploitation and preservation of the vested interests. And yet I knew well that there has something else in it, something which supplied a deeper inner craving of human beings. How else could it have been the tremendous power it has been and brought peace and comfort to innumerable souls? I am afraid it is impossible for me to seek anchorage in this way; I prefer the open sea with all its storms and tempests. Nor am I greatly interested in the after life, in what happens after death. I find the problems of life sufficiently absorbing to fill my mind. The traditional Chinese outlook has appeal for me ...... how to understand life, not to reject it but to accept it, to conform to it and to improve it.

(185 words)

Precis

Title : *Life and Religion*

The writer says that he is more interested in understanding life with its myriad problems at it is. But at the same time religion has also interested him which, inspite of all the evils associated with it, has given solace to the craving mind, otherwise how could it have had so much of influence and brought peace and comfort to human mind. India, as a religious country bears testimony to this fact. *(70 words)*

(Now in this passage the writer begins by talking about religion and all the evils associated with it, bigotry, dogma and superstition but the central idea is life with its myriad problems; religion is the second and subsidiary point. So in the precis the order of ideas has been so arranged.

Moreover, the passage is the opinion given by the writer in the first person which has been changed to the third person).

EXAMPLE 7

What manner was Napolean then? Was he one of the great ones of the earth, the Man of Destiny as he was called, a mighty hero and one who helped in freeing, humanity from its many burdens? Or was he, as H.G. Wells and some others say, a mere adventurer and a wrecker, who did great injury to Europe and civilisation? Probably both these views are exaggerated, probably both contain some measure of the truth. All of us are curious mixtures of the good and the bad, the great and the little. He was such a mixture; but unlike most of us, extraordinary qualities went to make up the mixture. He had courage, self-confidence, imagination, amazing energy and vast ambition. He was a very great general, a master of the art of war, comparable to the great captains of old — Alexander and Chengiz. But he was petty and selfish and self-centred and the dominating impulse of his life was not the pursuit of an ideal, but the quest of personal power. "My mistress!", he once said, "Power is my mistress! The conquest of that mistress has cost me so much that I will allow no one to rob me of her, or to share her with me". Child of the Revolution he was, and yet be dreamt of a vast Empire and the conquests of Alexander filled his mind. Even Europe seemed small. The East lured him and especially Egypt and India. "Only in the East", he said, early in his career when he was twenty-seven, "have there been great empires and mighty changes; in the east where six hundred million people dwell. Europe is a mole hill". *(274 words)*

(**Note.** This passage contains the character of Napolean. There are a couple of quotations from what Napolean said. In a precis nothing like these quotations are to be kept; only the main idea contained in them will be incorporated.

Further, the passage begins with interrogatory sentences. In a precis no such sentences in this form are to be put. The precis has to be simply in the affirmative sentences).

Precis

Title : *Character of Napolean—A Mixture of Opposites.*

Napolean's character is a mixtures of opposites. He was a great commander, possessed great imagination, courage and self-confidence. But he was too ambitious, power-hungry, and self-conceited. He wanted to conquer not only Europe but even the East; Egypt and India were on his plans of conquest. Europe alone appeared to him a tiny region for his vast conquests. He was a great conqueror but historians have also described him as a great wrecker who ruined the world and its civilisation.

(*82 words*)

EXAMPLE 8

There is something radically wrong with the entire structure of human relationship that makes men delight in killing man, whether it be in the name of civilization or religion or anything else. Two wrongs do not make a right; hatred must beget hatred; and what is brought into being by violence can and will always be destroyed by greater violence. It is this fundamental truth that women have got to bring home to the people in their respective countries. No peace treaties can avail that have revenge as their basis and a self-righteous arrogance and hypocrisy in the so-called victors. Women are the natural preserve of life. Life grows from within them. They could make their influence felt if they would be big enough to rise above the walls of narrow nationalism that confine us today. Just as communism calls the workers of the world to unite, let the women of the world unite and stake all for a life worth living. Love conquers all things. We have it in us to give. If we could only realize our moral strength and non-cooperate with violence in whatsoever from it raises its head — the womanhood can be the saviour of the world community. (*198 words*)

(**Note.** Although the passage begins by talking about violence and hatred in any form or on any account but the central thought on which the whole matter concentrates is the role of women is establishing peace in the violence–ridden world. They can be the initiates and the harbingers of peace and the precis has to catch this point first; other ideas would follow subsequently and would be adjuncts to the central idea.

This is what the effort of a precis writer should be to catch the crux first).

Precis

Title : *Role of Women*

In this conflict and violence ridden world, women can play a vital role in ridding the world of this malaise. They can make use of their influence in the family of which they are the progenator and they teach the progenator and they can teach and preach the lesson that hatred would bring hatred. Let the women of the world unite in this campaign to bring about unity and peace in the world which no peace-treaties can bring about.

(*70 words*)

EXAMPLE 9

Perhaps we are living in one of the great ages of mankind and have to pay the price for that privilege. For the great ages have been full of conflicts and instability, of an attempt to change over from the old to something new. There is not permanent stability and security and changelessness for then life itself would cease. At the most we can seek a relative stability and a moving equilibrium. Life is a continuous struggle on the physical, intellectual and moral plane out of which new things take shape and fresh ideas are born. Destruction and construction go side by side and both aspects of man and nature are ever evident. Life is a principle of growth, not of standing still, a continuous becoming which does not permit static conditions. (*130 words*)

Precis

Title : *Change*

Change is the law of nature. All great ages have hankered for a change. Without change life would cease to exist. Constant struggle on all planes is going on for new things to take shape. Life grows out of extinction.

(*40 words*)

EXAMPLE 10

Like every other instrument that man has invented, sport can be used for good or for evil purposes. Used well, it can teach endurance and courage, a sense of fair play and a respect for rules, coordinated effort and the subordination of personal interests to those of the group. Used badly, it can encourage personal vanity and group vanity, great desire for victory and hatred for rivals and intolerant esprit de corps and contempt for people who are beyond a certain arbitrary selected pole. Sport can be either a preparation for war or, in some measure, a substitute for war; a training ground either of potential war-managers or of potential peace-lovers; an educative influence forming either militarists or men who will be ready and able to apply the principle of pacifism in every activity of life. If is for us to choose which part of the organised amusements of children and adults shall play.

(*152 words*)

Precis

Title : *The Plus and Minus Roles of Sports*

Sports is an activity created by men which can create good men or evil men. Endurance, courage, a sense of fair play are the plus qualities that sports encourage to develop while vanity, greed to win and rivalry are its minus points. In sports lie the seeds of war preparedness or love for peace and goodwill. (*52 words*)

ONE-WORD SUBSTITUTION

ONE-WORD SUBSTITUTION

Having taken lessons in Precis Writing, it becomes necessary how words can be condensed in the shortest form, how the content of a number of words can be contained just in one word. This condensation of an idea in one-word can go a long way in precis writing and limiting the length of the precis. One-word substitution, in this way becomes an essential part in the process of Precis writing and with that end in view one-word which can stand for a number of words — their list is being given herewith. Though, of course, no list can be exhaustive, but then as many one-words which can cover the general set of words normally and usually used in our daily intercourse have been enlisted.

To quote a few examples — 'A handwriting which cannot easily be read' — can be expressed in one-word 'Illegible'. 'A child born of an illegal marriage or no marriage' — will be 'Illegitimate'; 'A document drawn up with false signatures' would be called 'forged'. These are just sample examples.

1. One who knows everything or sees everything. — *Omniscient*
2. One who is all powerful. — *Omnipotent*
3. One who is present everywhere. — *Omnipresent* (God is omnipresent)
4. One who always looks at the dark side of things. — *Pessimist*

5. One who looks at the bright side of things. — *Optimist*

6. One who cannot read or write. — *Illiterate*

7. One (a child) who is born after the death of his father. — *Posthumous*

8. A work published or an award given after the death of the writer or the death of the awardee. — *Posthumous*

9. A letter or any writing whose writer is unknown. — *Anonymous*

10. Government by one. — *Autocracy*

11. Government by the people. — *Democracy*

12. Government by a king. — *Monarchy*

13. Government by the nobility. — *Aristocracy*

14. Government by the officials. — *Bureaucracy*

15. Government by a few. — *Oligarchy*

16. Government by the rich. — *Plutocracy*

17. One who believes in God. — *Theist*

18. One who does not believe in god. — *Atheist*

19. That which can be eaten. — *Edible*

20. That which cannot be eaten. —*Inedible*

21. A handwriting which cannot easily be read. —*Illegible*

22. One who cannot be corrected or reformed. —*Incorrigible*

23. One who or which cannot be conquered. —*Invincible*

24. Work or job done without receiving any remuneration. —*Honorary*

25. A job which offers no remuneration.— *Sinecure*

26. To talk impiously about pious things. — *Blaspheme*

27. Men living or things happening at one time or period. — *Contemporary*

28. One who has no means to pay his debts. —*Insolvent*

29. One who hates women. — *Misogynist*

30. A remedy for all ills. — *Panacea*

31. One who is indifferent to pleasure or pain. — *Stoic*

32. A man with a long experience of service or occupation. — *Veteran*

33. One who is too fiercely in favour of his views or religion. —*Fanatic*

34. To think over some problem carefully. — *Ponder*

35. Animals equally at home on land and water. — *Amphibious*

36. One who turns some one into an enemy. —*Alienate*

37. One who is liked by one and all. — *Popular*

38. The life history of a man written by somebody. — *Biography*

39. The life history of a man written by his ownself. —*Autobiography*

40. A man interested in the welfare of women. — *Feminist*

41. One who hates mankind. —*Misanthrope*

42. One who is at home in all countries. — *Cosmopolitan*

43. A voice or sound which cannot be heard. — *Inaudible*

44. One who cannot be seen. — *Invisible*

45. One who cannot be defeated. — *Invincible*

46. That which cannot be believed. — *Incredible*

47. One who believes anybody and everybody. — *Credulous*

48. That which can be believed. — *Credible*

49. That which cannot be blotted out. — *Indelible* (impression or mark or blot)

50. That which cannot be satisfied. — *Insatiable* (hunger, desire, animation)

51. That which cannot be altered or withdrawn. — *Irrevocable*

52. That which is not likely to happen. — *Improbable*

53. That which cannot be explained. —*Inexplicable*

54. A loss or damage which cannot be compensated with. — *Irreparable*

55. That which cannot be initiated. — *Inimitable*

56. A first attempt on somebody's part. — *Maiden* (first speech, first feat)

57. Behaviour like that of woman. — *Effeminate*
58. Behaviour like that of a man. — *Masculine*
59. Behaviour like that of a child when used in a aderisive way) —*Childish*
Behaviour like that of a child when used in an appreciative way. — *Childlike*
60. Murder of a man. — *Homicide*
61. Murder of the father. — *Patricide*
62. Murder of the mother. — *Matricide*
63. Murder of the brother. — *Fratricide*
64. Murder of the king. — *Regicide*
65. Murder of one's ownself. — *Suicide*
66. A custom or a word out of use or no more in use. — *Obsolete*
67. Too much of official formality. — *Red-Tapism*
68. Animals which suckle their mothers. — *Mammals*
69. A decision taken by all those present. — *Unanimous*
70. Two or more things happening at the same time. —*Simultaneous*
71. Two or more persons living at the same time. — *Contemporary*
72. Something done of one's own free will. — *Voluntary*
73. Something required to be done under orders. — *Compulsory*

74. A match which remains undecided. — *Drawn*

75. The right of voting. — *Frenchise*

76. The voter in an election. — *Electorate*

77. A speech or action made or done at the spur of the moment. — *Extempore*
(without any previous preparation)

78. A place where weapons are stored. — *Arsenal*

79. A place where old and ancient historical records or things are kept and preserved. — *Museum*

80. An area where rare animals, beasts and birds are kept. — *Zoo*

81. A lover of women. — *Philogynist*

82. One who tries to make false love with different woman. — *Philanderer*

83. A person who put himself to physical hardships for the salvation of his soul. — *Ascetic*

84. One who prefers to remain unmarried and not indulge in sex. —*Celibate*

85. An act of remaining away from sex.— *Celibacy*

86. Marrying one or one wife at a time. — *Monogamy*

87. Marrying more than one wife or more than one husband at a time. — *Polygamy*

88. Marrying more than one husband at a time. — *Polyandry*

89. The act of doing undue favour of one's relatives through one's official position. — *Nepotism*

90. One who loves his fellowmen and serves them. — *Philanthropist*

91. One who can use both his hands with equal effect. — *Ambhidexterous*

92. A close-fisted stingy person. — *Niggard*

93. One who has an undue love of money or wealth or possessions. — *Greedy*

94. An ill-timed action or speech. — *Inopportune*

95. One who never fails. (a remedy, an action). — *Infallible*

96. A harmless person, action or anything. — *Innocuous*

97. A tendency to show undue favour, or to lean on one side unduly. — *Partiality*

98. An order or judgement which is absolutely clear. — *Unambiguous*

99. Liable to be called upon to explain. — *Answerable*

100. A person representing a government or an authority on the diplomatic level. — *Ambassador*

101. The original inhabitants of a region or a country. — *Aboriginals*

102. To give up the throne or office of dignity or authority. — *Abdicate*

103. One who is a narrow-mined and prejudiced in his religious views. — *Bigot*

104. A woman with a fair complexion and light coloured hair. — *Blonde*

105. A woman with dark complexion and brown hair. — *Brunette*

106. One who is always inclined to fight.— *Bellicose*

107. One who is equally competent in two languages. — *Bilingual*

108. Animals equally at home in sea and land. — *Amphibious*

109. A man having no sense of sympathy.— *Callous*

110. Persons working together in one office or one organisation. — *Colleagues*

111. Want of rain. — *Drought* (pronounced as Drowt)

112. A gulp of water or drink. — *Draught*

113. Extreme old age when a man behave foolishly. — *Dotage*

114. An action or speech with a doubtful intent. — *Dubious*

115. Fit or worthy of some job, marriage etc. — *Eligible*

116. One who always thinks of his own interests or too high of himself. — *Egoist*

117. One who always talks of himself. — *Egotist*

118. One who indulges in luxuries of the table or of sensual pleasure. — *Epicure*

119. A social out cast. — *Pariah*

120. The science that deals with the origin and history of words. — *Etymology*

121. To root out some disease, or rot or evil. — *Eradicate*

122. A man having uncommon and unusual habits or behaviours. — *Eccentric*

123. One who acts or speaks without pre-thought. — *Impetuous*

124. A man with habits difficult to be met or satisfied. — *Fastidious*

125. That which destroys germs. — *Germicide*

126. Remarks or subjects which have no connection with what is being discussed, talked about or written. — *Irrelevant*

127. A person who cannot be tired out in his efforts. — *Indefatigable*

128. Worships of images or idols. — *Idolatory*

129. One who destroys the images or idols or even old ideas or beliefs. — *Iconoclast*

130. To light up with lights or to throw new light on certain issues. — *Illuminate*

131. To explain something in detail. — *Elucidate*

132. To urge or encourage a person to do some evil act. — *Instigate*

133. One who suffers from nervous disorder. — *Neurotic*

134. One who suffers from heart problems. — *Cardiac*

135. An object to be kept in memory. — *Momento*

136. One who keeps dependent an another for nutrition or living. — *Parasite*
(It can be a person, a plant, a cell, an insect, a creature)

137. Examination of the body after death. — *Post-mortem*

138. A place where dead bodies are kept before cremation or burial. — *Mortuary*

139. A writer who copies out from the writings of others — ideals, words, or findings. — *Plagiarist*

140. Something—object, place, even thought or plan beyond possibility. — *Remote*

141. Violating the sanctity of something. — *Sacrilege*

142. To make safe from germs or infection. — *Sterilize*

143. Reproducing something — words for word. — *Verbatim*

144. One who eats only vegetables and abstains from meat. — *Vegetarian*

145. Animals who live in flocks. — *Gregarious*

146. Animals which lives in water — *Aquatic*

147. Animals with two feet. — *Biped*

148. Animals with four feet. — *Quadruped*

149. A person who knows several languages — *Linguist*

150. That which kills germs and infections. — *Antiseptic*

151. One who eats too much. — *Glutton*

152. One who spends too much. — *Spendthrift*

153. One who tries to spend less and less as lesser as possible. — *Miser*
(money miser, miserly words, expressions can be used for all these too)

154. That which can be clearly seem through. — *Transparent*
(This term can be used for things as well as for thoughts and actions)
'His thoughts are most transparent; his actions have full transparency'.

155. That which cannot be penetrated through, or conquered.
— *Invulnerable, Impregnable, Unconquerable*

156. One who or what is easily amendable to be won over, or which has weak points or can be easily won over. — *Vulnerable*

157. One who walks in sleep. — *Somnambulist*

158. A voice which cannot easily be heard. — *Inaudible*

159. Writings or any shows which express or exhibit more of sex. — *Pornography*

160. As person who dies without making a will. — *Inestate*

161. Drowsiness inducing drugs. — *Narcotic*

162. Study of insects. — *Entomology*

163. A tank where fishes or water creatures are kept. — *Aquarium*

164. One who is doing things just for money. — *Mercenary*

(Soldiers fighting just for money, not for any cause)

165. Estate inherited from ancestors. — *Patrimony*

166. One who speaks to others for a party. — *Spokesman*

167. One who changes principles, sides, or parties. — *Turncoat*

168. One who eats human flesh. — *Cannibal*

169. One who thinks that human nature is essentially evil. — *Cynic*

170. One who doubts if God exists or not. — *Agnostic*

171. One who is not a professional but just does something for pleasure. — *Amateur*

172. That which cannot be repaired. — *Irreparable*

173 A decision or action which cannot be turned back. — *Irrevocable*

174. One who walks on foot. — *Pedestrian*

175. That which can easily catch fire.— *Inflammable*

176. Actions which have political intent and manipulations. — *Diplomacy*

177. A compilation of any type of literature. — *Anthology*

178. Destroying works of art by violent means. — *Vandalism*

179. A person who is good judge of a piece of art, of food, of wine etc. — *Connoisseur*

180. One who has been appointed of settle a dispute. — *Arbitrator*

181. A notice issued on the death of somebody. — *Obituary*

182. A poem written on the death of somebody. — *Elegy*

183. Words inscribed on a tomb. — *Epitaph*

184. One who has knowledge of several talents or arts. — *Versatile*

185. One who abstains from wine. —*Teetotaller*

186. One who is new to any business. — *Novice*

187. Book containing information on all subjects. — *Encyclopaedia*

188. Place for keeping birds. — *Aviary*

189. China clay tea-cups, plates, saucers, etc. — *Crockery*

190. Knives, forks etc. used for eating. — *Cutlery*

191. An almirah to keep things —with drawers etc. — *Cupboard*

192. One who believes in establishing peace. — *Pacifist*

193. That which is easy to be carried from one place to another. — *Portable*

194. Water which is worthy for drinking. — *Potable*

195. Age between boyhood and youth.— *Adolescence*

196. That which lasts for sometime. — *Transitory*

197. That which has to last only for some time.
— *Evanescent*

198. That which cannot be copied or imitated.
— *Inimitable*

199. That which is against law. — *Illegal*

200. One who has no feeling for others. — *Callous*

201. One who feels happy at other's misery or misfortune. — *Saddist*

❑❑❑